COLLECTIVE AGRICULTURE AND RURAL DEVELOPMENT IN SOVIET CENTRAL ASIA

The World Employment Programme (WEP) was launched by the International Labour Organisation in 1969, as the ILO's main contribution to the International Development Strategy for the Second United Nations Development Decade.

The means of action adopted by the WEP have included the following:
- short-term high-level advisory missions;
- longer-term national or regional employment teams;
- and a wide-ranging research programme.

A landmark in the development of the WEP was the World Employment Conference of 1976, which proclaimed inter alia that 'strategies and national development plans should include as a priority objective the promotion of employment and the satisfaction of the basic needs of each country's population'. The Declaration of Principles and Programme of Action adopted by the Conference have become the cornerstone of WEP technical assistance and research activities during the closing years of the Second Development Decade.

This publication is the outcome of a WEP project.

COLLECTIVE AGRICULTURE AND RURAL DEVELOPMENT IN SOVIET CENTRAL ASIA

Azizur Rahman Khan
and
Dharam Ghai

A study prepared for the International Labour Office within the framework of the World Employment Programme

St. Martin's Press   New York

All rights reserved. For information write:
St. Martin's Press, Inc., 175 Fifth Avenue New York, N.Y. 10010
Printed in Great Britain
First published in the United States of America in 1980

ISBN 0–312–14975–1

Library of Congress Cataloging in Publication Data

Khan, Azizur Rahman.
    Collective agriculture and rural development in
Soviet central Asia.

    "A study prepared for the International Labour
Office within the framework of the World employ-
ment programme."
    Includes index.
    1. Collective farms—Soviet Central Asia.
2. Rural development—Soviet Central Asia.
I. Ghai, Dharam P., joint author. II. Interna-
tional Labor Office. III. Title.
HD1492.R92S728   1979   338.7′63′09584   79–15807
ISBN 0–312–14975–1

For Mohua and Neela

Contents

Preface

This monograph represents a part of the ongoing research project on alternative agrarian systems being carried out by the Rural Employment Policies Branch within the framework of the World Employment Programme of the ILO. This research project evaluates agrarian systems in terms of their contribution to increasing employment and production, reducing poverty, promoting an egalitarian distribution of income, generating surplus for self-sustained growth and mass participation. In this study the performance of the Soviet Central Asian collective agriculture is assessed. It is a very interesting case since for nearly five decades communal agriculture has served as the vehicle for transforming and developing what was a once poor and backward rural society.

In preparing this study the authors received a great deal of help from so many institutions and individuals that it is impossible to mention all of them. First and foremost they would like to thank the governments of the USSR and of the Tajik and Uzbek SSRs for granting permission for and organising a field visit to Tajikistan and Uzbekistan. In Moscow the authors received much assistance from the State Committee of Labour and Social Affairs of the Council of Ministers of the USSR (especially from Mr A. F. Bordadyn, the Chief of its Division of International Relations and Mr A. Kulagin who accompanied the authors to Tajikistan) and the Ministry of Agriculture (particularly Mr V. Ashomko who accompanied the authors to Uzbekistan). Professor Vladimir Venzher was kind enough to come out of retirement to have discussions with the authors. The ILO Branch Office in Moscow (especially its Director, Mr N. Korioukine and Messrs Solomonov and Borodavkin) made a material contribution to the preparation of this study by working closely with the Soviet authorities in organising the field visit and making other arrangements.

In Tajikistan Mr Narzibekov, the Chairman of the State Committee of Labour and Mr Zuraev, the Deputy Minister of Agriculture spent a lot of time with the authors and shared their vast experience and knowledge about the development of Soviet Central Asia. Mr Sahibnazarov, the Secretary of the All Republic Council of Kolkhozy in Tajikistan and Mr Hamroaliev, who acted as the interpreter, were always with the authors to explain things and to help in every possible way.

In Uzbekistan the authors' chief debt of gratitude is to Mr Khalikulov, Deputy Chairman of the State Committee of Labour and to Mr Pulatov of the Ministry of Agriculture. The authors would like to thank the members of the staff (especially Mr Kaiumov, the Deputy Director, Mr Galeev, who prepared a background paper and Mr Zakhirkhojaev) of the Central Asian Scientific Research Institute of Agricultural Economics at Tashkent for two very useful meetings. Mr Samatov, of the State Committee of Labour and Mr Yuldashov, the Minister of Agriculture, both of the Samarkand Oblast, were of very considerable assistance.

The authors would like to record the remarkable hospitality received at the five collective farms that they visited. For all their acts of kindness and many memorable events the authors would like to thank the Chairpersons of these collective farms: Mr Khaitov (Kolkhoz Karl Marx), Mr Baimuradov (Kolkhoz Rossiya), Mr Sharipov (Kolkhoz XXII Party Congress), Mr Isakov (Kolkhoz Leninism) and Mrs Annakulova (Kolkhoz Kholkabad).

At the ILO Headquarters the authors acknowledge with gratitude the moral and material support provided by Madame Antoinette Beguin, Chief of the Employment and Development Department. They also received helpful comments from Jacques Gaude, Vladimir Kondratiev, Stanislav Kouzmin, Eddy Lee, Harold Lubell, Jean Mouly, G. B. Ng, Peter Peek, Samir Radwan, Anisur Rahman and Gerry Rodgers. Norman Langford helped with the translation of terms. Frances Kaufmann and Sandra Berlinka typed and provided technical help in preparing the manuscript.

Keith Griffin of Queen Elizabeth House, Oxford, gave very

helpful comments. Saidur R. Lasker of the FAO helped with some data.

In conclusion it should be stressed that the responsibility for the views expressed and the inevitable errors that remain rests with the authors alone. Neither the ILO nor any of the persons and institutions named above have any share in it.

International Labour Office   A. R. Khan
December 1978   D. P. Ghai

The Soviet Central Asian Republics and their immediate neighbours

1 An Introduction

1. A BRIEF HISTORICAL BACKGROUND

The Soviet Central Asian economic region consists of four republics: Uzbekistan, Tajikistan, Turkmenistan and Kirghizia. The region is bounded by the Caspian Sea on the west, Iran and Afghanistan on the south, China on the east and the vast steppes of Soviet Kazakhstan on the north. Together the four republics have a territory of 1.28 million square kilometres and a population (in 1977) of 24.2 million. The average population density of 19 per square kilometre is misleading. Vast parts of the region consist of desert or mountains where very few people live. In the fertile river basin the density of population frequently exceeds 200 per square kilometre. Thus in Uzbekistan the density per square kilometre varies from 5 in the arid desert Karakalpak Autonomous Soviet Socialist Republic (ASSR) to 230 in Ferghana Oblast and 308 in Andijan Oblast.[1]

Uzbekistan is the largest (in terms of population) and the most advanced (in terms of economic development) of the four republics. It has an area of 447,400 square kilometres (approximately the size of Sweden) and a population (in 1977) of 14.47 millions (a little higher than that of Netherlands). Uzbekistan alone has 60 per cent of the population of Central Asia. Tajikistan, the next largest republic in terms of population, has an area of 143,100 square kilometres (about the same as Greece) and a population (in 1977) of 3.59 million (the same as that of Israel). Kirghizia is next in terms of population (3.44 million in 1977) with an area of 198,500 square kilometres. The biggest of the republics in terms of area (488,100 square kilometres) is Turkmenistan which has the lowest population (2.65 million in 1977).

Central Asia was annexed by Tsarist Russia in the second half

1

of the nineteenth century. Before being annexed by Russia, Turkestan (the old name of the territory that now forms the Central Asian Republics) was economically an overwhelmingly agricultural society dominated by large feudal landlords. Politically the region was fragmented mainly into three states – the Bukhara Emirate and the Kokand and Khiva Khanates. Socially the area was under the influence of the orthodox religious system of Islam.

The Russian conquerors did not try to alter the social and economic systems in any fundamental way. Indeed, they preferred to rule through the local feudal aristocracy. While the Kokand Khanate and some other territories were included directly into the Russian empire as Turkestan Governorate-General, the titular sovereignty of the vassal states of Bukhara and Khiva was recognised.

And yet the colonial rule of Tsarist Russia gradually brought about some far-reaching economic changes. The need to integrate the economies of the colonies led to the opening up of the railway transport connecting Central Asia with Russia. The Transcaspian line reached Samarkand by 1888 and the Orenburg line to Tashkent was completed by 1905. Following the opening up of the railway transport a large number of immigrants from Russia's internal regions moved into Central Asia. Together with the later waves of migration during the Soviet period this explains the relatively high proportion of Russians in these republics today.[2]

Another important economic change was the development of cotton production in Central Asia to supply raw material to the Russian textile industry. The Russian conquest of Central Asia coincided with the drying up of the traditional American source of cotton imports due to the civil war in the USA. Turkestan was converted into the principal supplier of cotton to Russia to fill in the gap.

Repercussions of the Russian Revolution of 1917 were felt in parts of Central Asia almost immediately. But it was not until 1920 that the overthrow of the Emirate of Bokhara and the Khanate of Khiva was completed. The present political boundaries were gradually drawn during the 1920s to form four republics, each representing a major nationality. Thus a clear rejection of the traditional basis of political entities was made in favour of the linguistic-cultural basis of the nation-hood of each republic. In reality each of the republics is a multinational entity.[3]

National delimitation of Central Asia was carried out in stages. In 1924 the Uzbek and the Turkmen Soviet Socialist Republics were formed as the constituent republics of the USSR.[4] At the time Uzbekistan did not incorporate the present Karakalpak ASSR (which continued to be an auto-nomous Oblast within what was then the Kazakh ASSR, itself an Autonomous Republic within the Russian Soviet Federated Socialist Republics – the RSFSR). Tajikistan, on the other hand, became an ASSR within the Uzbek SSR. Also at the time Kirghizia became the Kara-Kirghiz autonomous Oblast within the RSFSR. In 1929 Tajikistan became a full republic and in 1932 the present boundaries of Uzbekistan were completed by the transfer to it of the Karakalpak ASSR. In 1926 Kirghizia was given the status of an ASSR. In 1936 it became a full republic to complete the present national boundaries of the Central Asian region.

2. THE PURPOSE OF THE STUDY

A few decades ago Central Asia was an overwhelmingly rural and extremely poor society. In recent decades it has undergone a remarkable transformation. The rate at which it attained material progress has been remarkably high. In terms of social institutions there was a simultaneous transformation of unpre-cedented proportions. The rural society of the region was catapulted from the middle ages into modern collective farms and state farms at one go. Another interesting feature of the transformation of Central Asia is that the development of the rural economy was an integral part of the material advance-ment. As a result, the region continues to be predominantly rural.

All these features make it very interesting to analyse the Central Asian experience in agricultural and rural develop-ment in order to determine the factors that led to such a different performance in the region as compared to that of its immediate neighbours. Such an analysis should provide useful insights for the planning of agricultural and rural development in societies which today approximate the circumstances which existed in the Central Asian republics a few decades ago.

The main focus of the study is on the collective farms—the Kolkhoz—to determine their achievements from the standpoint of productive efficiency, egalitarianism of income distribution, generation of surplus and promotion of employment and participation. There is also some discussion of the organisation and management of collective farms. For purposes of comparison references will be made to the state farms—the Sovkhoz—and some discussion of the overall development strategy will be attempted in order to put the experience of collective agriculture in the appropriate context.

3. METHODOLOGY AND DATA

The information on which the study has been based comes from two main sources: published official data and the limited amount of data generated by the authors during a field trip in October 1977. The field trip was made to the republics of Uzbekistan and Tajikistan, the two most populous republics of the region. This is why in the study these two republics have received much greater attention than have their other two Central Asian neighbours.

During the field trip attention was concentrated on the collection of micro data in five collective farms especially on those aspects of their working on which little quantitative information is available from official sources. The purpose of generating information on the working of so few collective farms was not to try to make quantitative approximations of the characteristics of the Kolkhoz system on various aspects. To do so on the basis of such a tiny 'sample', which was not drawn on the basis of any scientific criteria, would make little sense. Our purpose was rather to derive some broad qualitative idea of how the system works with respect to certain features on which alternative sources of information are scanty. In interpreting the data reported for the five Kolkhoz this qualification must be kept in mind.

Gaps in statistical information will only be too obvious to

the reader. On many interesting issues we have, therefore, been able to do little more than raise questions or suggest hypotheses. To arrive at less tentative results one would have to await the availability of information on a whole range of issues related to this experience.

4. A PLAN OF THE STUDY

Chapter 2 provides a general overview of collective agriculture and its evolution in the broader context of agricultural and development strategies. Chapter 3 briefly describes the evolution of the Kolkhoz system and analyses its organisation and management. Chapter 4 is concerned mainly with the analysis of the productive efficiency of the Central Asian Kolkhoz. A brief discussion on internal accumulation in collective agriculture is also included. Chapter 5 provides an analysis of the distribution of income and collective consumption. Chapter 6 puts together the main pieces of information on the five Kolkhoz that the authors visited as part of their field trip. In the concluding chapter the major achievements and problems of Central Asian collective agriculture are summarised.

2 The Evolution of Agricultural and Development Policies in Soviet Central Asia: An Overall Perspective

1. INTRODUCTION

The purpose of this chapter is to provide a general overview of agricultural and broader development policies pursued in Soviet Central Asia and their effects in shaping the evolution of collective agriculture in the region. The emphasis will be on the distinctive features of agriculture and rural society in Central Asia, those which make the Central Asian experience so very different from the over-all Soviet one.

We shall begin with an analysis of the main demographic characteristics which are remarkably different from not only the USSR but also any other nation with a comparable living standard. These demographic features have powerful effects on general economic circumstances and policies. Next, we shall discuss the relatively lower rate of urbanisation in Central Asia as compared with the rest of the USSR and try to compare the causes and consequences of such difference in terms of living standards. Finally, we shall analyse the remarkably different orientation of Soviet economic policy towards Central Asian agriculture as compared with that towards agriculture in much of the rest of the USSR. We shall try to trace the very different results of these policies in Central Asia in comparison with those obtained in Soviet agriculture as a whole.

6

2. DEMOGRAPHIC FACTORS

Tables 2.1 and 2.2 summarise some of the basic demographic statistics for Central Asia as a whole and for Uzbekistan and Tajikistan. In 1913 the region constituted only 4.6 per cent of the total population of the area that now forms the USSR. By 1977 the share has more than doubled to 9.4 per cent. About the time of the revolution the rate of population growth in Central Asia was probably no higher than that in the USSR. Even by 1940 the Central Asian population growth rate was only a little higher than that for the rest of the USSR. But since then the demographic trends in Central Asia have diverged sharply from those in the rest of the Union. While the latter experienced a demographic transition through sharply reduced birth rates, the rate of population growth in the Central Asian republics continued to accelerate.

The main factor in this expansion has been the sharp reduction in death rate. At the time of the revolution the death rate was probably similar to, or higher than, that in the present-day developing Asian countries. Even as recently as in 1940 the weighted average of the death rates in the four Central Asian republics was as high as 14.5 per thousand. By 1970 it dropped dramatically to 6 per thousand, one of the lowest rates ever recorded in any country of the world. By 1977 the death rate in the region was slightly higher, 7.5 per thousand, but still significantly below the average for the USSR, Europe and North America.[1] This is a singular testimony to the rising living standard, expanding health services and the relative environmental harmony that the region has experienced in the recent decades.

In terms of birth rate the region is showing no signs of a demographic transition. The weighted average of birth rates in the four republics is 35.1 per thousand, about twice as high as in the USSR.[2] As shown in Table 2.2 the birth rates in Uzbekistan and Tajikistan have tended to rise over the recent decades. In Kirghizia the rate has remained stable (at about 31 per thousand) while in Turkmenistan it has declined very slightly (from 37 in 1940 to 35 in 1976 per thousand). For the region as a whole the trend is a slightly rising one.

TABLE 2.1: Population

Year	USSR			Central Asia			Uzbekistan			Tajikistan		
	Population in Million	% Rural	Natural Rate of Growth	Population in Thousand	% Rural	Natural Rate of Growth	Population in Thousand	% Rural	Natural Rate of Growth	Population in Thousand	% Rural	Natural Rate of Growth
1913	159.2	82	1.64	7274	81	–	4334	76	–	1034	91	–
1940	194.1	67	1.32	10906	75	1.91	6551	75	2.06	1525	81	1.65
1959	208.8	52	1.78	13682	65	–	8119	66	–	1981	67	–
1966	232.2	47	1.09	17487	63	2.86	10399	64	2.88	2556	64	3.02
1970	241.7	44	0.92	19792	62	2.75	11800	63	2.81	2900	63	2.84
1977	257.8	38	0.89	24161	60	2.76	14474	61	2.82	3591	64	2.97

Source: *Narodnoe Khozyaistvo SSSR, Za 60 Let*; hereafter referred to as NK SU 60.
Note: The Central Asian figures are the weighted averages for Uzbekistan, Tajikistan, Turkmenistan and Kirghizia. The growth rates shown for 1966 and 1977 are in fact those respectively for 1965 and 1976. These are the differences between birth and death rates.

TABLE 2.2: Birth, Death and Population Growth Rates

Year	Uzbekistan			Tajikistan		
	Birth per 1000	*Death per 1000*	*% Growth Rate*	*Birth per 1000*	*Death per 1000*	*% Growth Rate*
1940	33.8	13.2	2.06	30.6	14.1	1.65
1965	34.7	5.9	2.88	36.8	6.6	3.02
1970	33.6	5.5	2.81	34.8	6.4	2.84
1975	34.5	7.2	2.73	–	–	–
1976	35.3	7.1	2.82	38.2	8.5	2.97

Source: *Narodnoe Khozyaistvo Uzbekskoi SSR Za 60 Let*: hereafter referred to as NK Uz. 60. *Sovietski Tajikistan Za 50 Let*: hereafter referred to as ST 50. *NK SU 60.*

A full analysis of the explanation of the high birth rate is beyond the scope of this study. Such an explanation will have to go into the historical and cultural factors that continue to condition the behaviour of the people in this region. It would, however, be wrong to try to find an explanation solely or primarily in the anti-Malthusian posture of the official Soviet doctrine on population. In spite of the official promotion of such a doctrine the rest of the USSR experienced demographic transition through a reduction in birth rate (e.g., from 33 per thousand in 1940 to 15.7 per thousand in 1965 in the RSFSR). Instead, beyond the cultural factors, one should try to find an explanation in such factors as the very low cost of having a child (due to free maternity and health services, free kindergarten and education, extensive social services and child allowances and predominance of rural life), assured income and employment prospects and the high demand for labour.[3]

The resulting natural rate of growth of population – 2.8 per cent per year in 1976 for the region as a whole – is one of the highest in the contemporary world and completely out of line as compared with nations with similar living standards. The actual rate of growth in population has been even greater due to net immigration. In Uzbekistan the actual annual rate of growth in the decade since 1966 has been 3.05 per cent per year which is higher than the annual average natural rate of growth in the republic over the same period.

The high birth rate and population growth have important economic and social consequences. The age distribution is skewed relatively sharply in favour of the children below working age. As is illustrated in Table 2.3 in Tajikistan the percentage of population below the age of 15 years is nearly two-thirds higher than that for the USSR. Consequently, the proportion of population in the potential labour force (which we have defined somewhat arbitrarily to include all persons between the ages 15 and 65 years) is lower. For every 100 people the USSR, on the average, has about 30 per cent more persons in the potential labour force than does Tajikistan. The situation in this regard in the other Central Asian republics is only marginally better than in Tajikistan.

TABLE 2.3: A Comparison of Age Distribution in Selected Areas

	Percentage of Population below the Age of 15	Percentage of Population between Ages 15 and 65
Tajikistan (1970)	47	49
USSR (1970)	29	63
Europe (1970)	25	64
South Asia (1970)	43	54
India (1970)	42	55
China (1970)	34	60

Source: *ST 50. NK SU 60*. ILO, *Labour Force Estimates and Projections*.

Even when compared with the developing countries of South Asia, including India, the Central Asian republics appear to be at a disadvantage from the standpoint of the age distribution of the population. In India and elsewhere in South Asia a significantly smaller proportion of the population is below the age of 15 years and a significantly higher proportion of the population is in the age group that we have defined to be the potential labour force.

The difference in the actual labour force tends to be even greater due to the limitation imposed on the participation of women in the labour force by the high birth rates and large families. As is illustrated by Table 2.4 women as a proportion of workers and white-collar workers (who do not include

TABLE 2.4: Women as Percentage of Workers and White Collar Workers:
1976

USSR	51
Uzbekistan	43
Tajikistan	38
Turkmenistan	40
Kirghizia	48

Source: *NK SU 60*

Kolkhoz workers) is much lower in Central Asia than in the
USSR as a whole.[4] As we shall report later, in the Kolkhoz the
number of days worked by a female worker is much lower than
that worked by an average male worker. An analysis of birth
rate and women as a percentage of the labour force in the 15
republics of the USSR in 1976 shows that there exists a highly
significant negative statistical relation between the variables –
the correlation coefficient is -0.88.

The total effect of the above factors is to provide the Central
Asian region with a much lower ratio of labour force to
population as compared to the USSR (or, for that matter, any
country that is comparable to Central Asia in terms of
economic development). As shown in Table 2.5, for every 100
persons the USSR has 45 per cent (56 per cent) more workers
than does Uzbekistan (Tajikistan).[5] As a consequence the
Central Asian republics have a much higher dependency ratio
than does the rest of the USSR. This is a very significant factor
in understanding the economic circumstances in the Central
Asian republics. Gains made in terms of income and productivity per worker in comparison with both the past and the
rest of the USSR are partly offset by the unfavourable
dependency ratio that obtains in this region.

On the eve of the revolution the level of urbanisation in
Central Asia was no lower than for the area that later became
the USSR. Indeed the territory that now forms Uzbekistan
was more urbanised than the then territories of any other
republic except Georgia.[6] During the period of Soviet power,
Central Asia experienced a much lower rate of urbanisation
than did the USSR as a whole. By the middle of the 1970s
Moldavia (with an urban population of 38 per cent of total)
was the only republic of the USSR that resembled the Central

TABLE 2.5: Kolkhozniki*, Workers and White Collar Workers as Percentage of Population

	1970	1976
USSR	44.2	46.6
Uzbekistan	31.1	32.1
Tajikistan	29.3	29.8

Note: These three categories constitute the bulk of the labour force though they do not account for the entire labour force. Thus, the ILO estimate for labour force as percentage of population in the USSR in 1970 is 48.48 (see ILO, *Labour Force Estimates and Projections*, Vol. IV). As far as we can establish the difference is due mainly to the exclusion of defence forces and certain other categories of public administrative services in the above estimates taken from official sources. The ILO estimates make allowance for these categories. We confine ourselves to the categories shown in the table because these are the only estimates available for the republics that are comparable with any all USSR estimate.

* Plural of Kolkhoznik. Similarly Kolkhozy and Sovkhozy are respectively the plural forms of the words Kolkhoz and Sovkhoz.

Asian republics in the predominance of the rural society. In every other republic the size of the urban population had exceeded the size of the rural population.

The immigrants into Central Asia largely settled in the urban areas. This is evidenced by a much higher proportion of the non-Central Asian population in the cities than in the country.[7] When one combines the fact of low rate of urbanisation with the high rate of immigration from outside into the cities, one reaches the conclusion that the rural-urban migration within the region was remarkably little. This is another important characteristic of Central Asian development to which we shall return later.

3. INDUSTRIAL GROWTH

The lower rate of urbanisation of Central Asia during the Soviet period must be interpreted carefully. As we shall try to argue later, it would be wrong to explain the phenomenon only with reference to a lack of pull from the industrial and urban centres. A good part of the explanation must be found in the relative lack of a powerful push out of the rural areas.[8]

Industrialisation got under way in the 1930s through the processing of cotton and other raw materials, e.g. silk, leather and wool. Already by 1940 the region produced 117 million metres of cotton textiles compared to an insignificant amount before revolution. In the pre-war years a solid basis was laid for the development of economic overheads by the electrification and geological explorations in the region. In the postwar period the industrial programme in the region received a major boost through the discovery that, contrary to the earlier belief that it had a deficient fuel balance, Central Asia was rich in gas, oil and water power. Large gas strikes were made in Uzbekistan and West Turkmenistan in the early 1960s. Also at this time the enormity of the hydroelectric potential of the region began to be fully realised. Tajikistan occupies the second place among all the republics of the USSR for its hydroelectric resources. During the post-war period, a more diversified and balanced industrial programme was implemented in the region. To give an example, the region now not only makes all the machinery for the cultivation of cotton and manufacturing of cotton textiles, but also exports many of them to a large number of destinations including India, Indonesia, Western Europe and the USA.

Table 2.6 summarises the rates of growth in industrial production in the four Central Asian republics as well as in the USSR as a whole.[9] By any ordinary standard the growth rates in Central Asia have been impressive. But they have generally been lower than the industrial growth rates in all USSR during each of the three time periods shown in the table. In

TABLE 2.6: Annual Compound Rates of Growth of Industrial Production

	Between 1913 and 1940	Between 1940 and 1965	Between 1965 and 1976
USSR	7.9	8.6	8.2
Uzbekistan	5.9	7.7	7.6
Tajikistan	8.4	7.8	7.7
Turkmenistan	7.3	6.2	8.4
Kirghizia	8.8	9.8	10.8

Source: The data on the basis of which these rates have been calculated are shown in *NK SU 60*.

Uzbekistan, the biggest and the most advanced of the republics, the rate of industrial growth has consistently been lower than in the USSR as a whole. The same result obtained in Tajikistan (except in the earliest period) and in Turkmenistan (except during the last decade). Only in Kirghizia has the rate of industrial growth been consistently higher than in the USSR.

Table 2.7 compares national income, its sectoral composition and per capita income in Uzbekistan with the

TABLE 2.7: National Income, Its Composition and Per Capita Income and Consumption

Uzbekistan

	1965	1970	1975	1976
National income (current price mill. rubles)	5495.9	8702.5	12483.1	13191.6
% Share of industry	37	34	38	40
% Share of agriculture	38	37	32	30
% Share of transport, construction trade and services	25	29	30	30
Per capita national income (current price)	544	738	912	937
Per capita consumption	412	543	675	698

USSR

	1965	1970	1975	1976
National income (Th. million rubles)	193.5	289.9	363.3	382.0
% Share of industry	52	51	53	53
% Share of agriculture	23	22	17	17
% Share of transport construction and services	25	27	30	30
Per capita national income	843	1199	1434	1495
Per capita consumption	611	833	1052	1095
Uzbek per capita national income as % of USSR's	64.5	61.6	63.6	62.7
Uzbek per capita consumption as % of USSR's	67.4	65.2	64.2	63.7

Source: *NK Uz. 60. NK SU 60.*

corresponding measurements for the USSR during the decade since 1965. In both, the share of agriculture in national income declined rapidly.[10] But the rate of decline was significantly greater for the USSR than for Uzbekistan. By 1976 the percentage share of agriculture in national income in Uzbekistan was three-quarters higher than that in the USSR. Correspondingly, the share of industry in national income in Uzbekistan is lower than that in the USSR. The comparison between the rest of Central Asia and the USSR will give results which are qualitatively similar.

4. TRENDS IN SECTORAL INCOMES

Table 2.7 shows that the per capita income in Uzbekistan in recent years has varied between 62 and 65 per cent of the per capita income for the USSR.[11] The disparity in terms of per capita consumption has been slightly lower. Tables 2.8 and 2.9 give some additional information about sectoral income comparison.

Table 2.8 compares payment per man-day in Kolkhoz in Uzbekistan and Tajikistan with that in the USSR as a whole.[12] The most striking feature is that by 1965 payment in Central Asia was more than a fifth higher than that in the USSR as a whole. Indeed, data available from an alternate source[13] indicate that in 1958 payment per man-day in the Central

TABLE 2.8: Payment Per Man-day in Kolkhoz

	All USSR (rubles)	Uzbekistan (rubles)	Tajikistan (rubles)	Uzbekistan as % of USSR	Tajikistan as % of USSR
1965	2.68	3.29	3.21	123	120
1970	3.90	4.24	4.17	109	107
1972	–	–	4.10	–	–
1973	–	–	4.37	–	–
1975	4.54	4.60	–	101	–
1976	4.77	4.96	–	104	–

Source: *NK SU 60*. *NK Uz. 60*. *ST 50*.

TABLE 2.9 Monthly Payment in Industry and State Agriculture

	Monthly Payment to Employees in Uzbekistan as % of that in USSR			Monthly Payment to Employees in Tajikistan as % of that in USSR	
	Industry	State Agriculture		Industry	State Agriculture
1940	81	104	1965	89	100
1965	90	92	1970	90	88
1970	93	97			
1975	94	96			
1976	92	94			

Source: These calculations are based on wages data shown in:
    NK SU 60, (p. 472) for the USSR, *NK Uz. 60* (p. 217) for Uzbekistan and *ST 50* (p. 190) for Tajikistan.
Note: 'State agriculture' refers to Sovkhoz and other (numerically less important) state enterprises in the agricultural sector.

Asian Kolkhoz was 70 per cent above that for the USSR as a whole.

Thus we have the important fact that, around the mid-1950s the Kolkhoz workers' collective earnings in Central Asia had reached a very high level in relation to that for the USSR. Unfortunately, we do not have the comparable data for the earlier years. But according to all available evidence the Central Asian agriculture in the early 1930s was less prosperous than the agriculture in most parts of the USSR. It would, therefore, be reasonable to assume that the disparity in Kolkhoz payments between Central Asia and the rest of the USSR started developing in favour of the former after these early years.

Over the years since the mid-1950s, the disparity between Central Asia and the USSR in terms of the earnings of the Kolkhoz workers has been narrowing down. By the middle of the 1970s the disparity virtually disappeared.

In Table 2.9 the earnings disparity in state agriculture (predominantly Sovkhoz) is shown. Once again, in the early years (e.g. 1940) the payment in Central Asia was higher than average. In more recent years the disparity has been reversed in favour of the rest of the USSR. One important fact to note is that regional disparity in payment in state agriculture is smaller than that in Kolkhoz payment.

When one looks at the regional disparity in industrial earnings, one finds a very different trend. In the earlier years the earnings in the Central Asian industries were relatively low as compared with the rest of the USSR. Over the years this disparity has been narrowing down, but, even in the 1970s, the earnings in the Central Asian industries remain significantly lower.

To summarise: by 1970 the collective earnings per worker from Kolkhoz in Central Asia were still somewhat higher than in the rest of the USSR, although the disparity had come down from about 70 per cent in 1958 to less than 10 per cent. The earnings in state agriculture had by 1970 already become higher in the rest of the USSR than in Central Asia. Since earnings in Sovkhoz are higher than those in Kolkhoz and since the USSR has a higher share of Sovkhoz in total agriculture as compared to Central Asia the weighted average earning per agricultural worker in Central Asia was probably only a shade higher than that in the rest of the USSR.[14] But the dependency ratio in rural Central Asia was way above that in the USSR as a whole. As a consequence *per capita* agricultural income in Central Asia was much lower than that in the USSR.[15] Earnings per industrial worker were lower in Central Asia and this disadvantage was further aggravated by the unfavourable dependency ratio so that the *per capita* industrial income in Central Asia was much lower than that in the USSR. To this one should add the fact that the USSR has a higher share of industry—the high income sector—in total economic activity. The total effect of all these factors is to reduce the per capita national income and per capita consumption in Central Asia to about two-thirds of the corresponding quantities in the USSR as a whole.[16]

Personal and household income in the USSR today amounts to no more than three quarters of the potentially consumable (or spendable) income at the disposal of the private individuals. The remainder is made up by the payments out of the Public Consumption Fund. A part of it consists of cash payments such as pensions and family allowances. But the bulk of it is paid in kind in the form of medical service, education, house rent subsidy and similar items. Table 2.10 shows per capita payments out of this fund in the USSR as a whole and in Uzbekistan and Tajikistan in selected years. Presumably the figures refer to the value of these services at cost, i.e., the cost incurred by the state. Per capita payment is lower in Central Asia than in the USSR as a whole, but this differential is somewhat lower in percentage term than that in per capita consumption and income. Thus socially provided consumption would appear to be acting as a mildly equalising factor in compensating for the regional differences in income and consumption.[17]

TABLE 2.10: Payment From Public Consumption Fund (rubles per head per year)

	1940	1965	1970	1975	1976
USSR	24	182	263	354	370
Uzbekistan	–	126	192	260	269
USSR as % of USSR per capita national income	–	22	22	25	25
Uzbekistan as % of Uzbekistan per capita national income	–	23	26	29	29
Uzbekistan as % of USSR	–	69	73	73	73
	1960	1965	1970	1972	1973
Tajikistan	83.5	124.9	178.1	202.4	215.1
Tajikistan as % of USSR	–	69	68	–	–

Source: *NK SU 60, p. 488. NK Uz. 60, p. 215. ST 50, p. 187.*

This may be the place to discuss very briefly the major achievements made by Central Asia in such areas as education, health and social securities. Unfortunately, we do not have separate figures for the rural areas so that the comparative progress in the USSR and the Central Asian republics has to be discussed in terms of overall figures for each. Tables 2.11 and 2.12 provide some basic facts.

The remarkable achievements in Central Asia stand out particularly clearly in comparison with the situation in the contemporary developing world. Compared to a literacy rate of about 20 per cent in the Indian sub-continent virtually

TABLE 2.11: Literacy Rates

(per cent)

	1897	1926	1939	1959	1970
USSR					
Total	28.4	56.6	87.4	98.5	99.7
Male	40.3	71.5	93.5	99.3	99.8
Female	16.6	42.7	81.6	97.8	99.7
Uzbekistan					
Total	3.6	11.6	78.7	98.1	99.7
Male	5.6	15.3	83.6	99.0	99.8
Female	1.2	7.3	73.3	97.3	99.6
Tajikistan					
Total	2.3	3.8	82.8	96.2	99.6
Male	3.9	6.4	87.4	98.0	99.8
Female	0.3	0.9	77.5	94.6	99.4

Source: *Narodnoe obrazovanic Nauka (Vladimis) i Kultura vSSSR* (Moskva, 1977), pp. 9–10.

complete literacy was achieved in Uzbekistan and Tajikistan in the late 1950s. Compared with about 3 doctors per 10,000 people in Asia and about 6.5 in Latin America the corresponding density in Central Asia is well over 20.[18]

Table 2.12 shows that the major reduction in disparity between the USSR and Central Asia took place between 1940 and 1965. Since 1965 the process has been slower and, indeed, some reversals with respect to certain elements have taken place. For example, in terms of students in higher education the difference between the USSR and Uzbekistan and in terms of hospital beds the difference between the USSR on the one hand and Uzbekistan and Tajikistan on the other increased between 1965 and 1976 in geometric terms. In arithmetic terms the difference widened with respect to the availability of doctors. These trends are generally consistent with income trends discussed above.[19]

There has been a steady improvement in overall and minimum pensions, sickness and disability allowances. Of particular importance is the change in the social security coverage for the collective farmers initiated in 1965 (all over

TABLE 2.12: Progress of Education and Health in Central Asia and the USSR

		1940	1965	1970	1976
Number of students in	USSR	41	166	188	192
higher education per	Uzbekistan	28	159	192	176
ten thousand persons	Tajikistan	15	119	149	145
Number of students in	USSR	50	158	180	179
medium level specialist	Uzbekistan	37	99	135	136
schools per ten thou- sand persons	Tajikistan	38	90	118	107
Number of doctors per	USSR	8	24	27	34
ten thousand persons	Uzbekistan	5	17	20	26
	Tajikistan	4	15	16	22
Number of medium level	USSR	24	73	87	100
medical staff per ten	Uzbekistan	18	52	65	80
thousand persons	Tajikistan	17	42	52	63
Number of hospital	USSR	40	96	109	119
beds per ten thousand	Uzbekistan	30	92	102	105
persons	Tajikistan	29	88	98	96

Source: *NK SU 60*. For the education statistics the figures refer to respective *financial years* starting in the calendar years shown.

the USSR). Prior to that date each Kolkhoz was responsible for pension schemes and other social welfare benefits for its members which differed between one Kolkhoz and another and were generally lower than those enjoyed by the workers of Sovkhoz. From 1965 social security benefits for all collective farms were unified and through a series of subsequent measures (e.g., lowering of retirement age to 60 years for men and to 55 years for women and the raising of overall and minimum pensions) these benefits were brought much closer to those enjoyed by the workers in state farms. Since collective farmers constitute a higher proportion of the labour force in Central Asia than in the rest of the USSR, these changes have meant more significant improvement there.

5. AN EXCEPTION TO THE STRATEGY OF PRIMITIVE SOCIALIST ACCUMULATION

We noted above that over approximately the two decades from the mid-1930s to the mid-1950s agricultural incomes grew much faster in Central Asia than in the rest of the USSR. We also noted that thereafter the rate of growth in agricultural incomes slowed down in Central Asia in relation to that in the rest of the USSR. We shall try to outline the main reasons behind these trends.

In development literature the Soviet experience is frequently characterised as the strategy of 'primitive socialist accumulation' – extracting large surplus from the agricultural sector by imposing on it unfavourable terms of trade through the use of the monopsonistic power of the state as the buyer of the agricultural goods and the monopolistic power of the state as the seller of non-agricultural goods. Indeed, the use of the monopsonistic power was not enough; the state had to impose compulsory delivery quotas on the rural producers. The main justification for the strategy was the lack of an alternative source of capital to finance socialist industrialisation in a pre-capitalist country in which socialist revolution had taken place.[20]

It appears that the main Central Asian cash crop, cotton, was no exception to this strategy in the very early years. The price offered to the growers was very low and, as a consequence, output fell. Trends in production and yield are expressed by the following figures for Uzbekistan:

Year	Production of raw cotton: thousand tons	Per hectare output in tons
1913	517.2	1.22
1924	205.8	0.78
1928	533.3	0.91
1930	744.3	0.84
1932	785.8	0.79

It was not too difficult, especially once collectivisation got under way, to increase area under cotton and, thereby to raise production to the pre-revolution peak and beyond. But the disincentive of low price was too strong an impediment to promote the necessary effort to restore the yield per hectare to anything like the pre-revolution level. It continued to decline and by 1932 output per hectare was 35 per cent below the level in 1913.[21]

For a period attempts were made to compensate the cotton growers by offering them grain, tea, sugar, seeds and fertiliser at fixed prices. In January 1935 these deliveries at fixed prices were discontinued and a major shift in policy was initiated by nearly quadrupling the procurement price of cotton. The result, in terms of production and yield, was dramatic – by 1937, in Uzbekistan, the production of raw cotton was 1522 thousand tons – nearly three times the pre-revolution peak— and yield per hectare was at an all time high of 1.6 tons. The result in the rest of Central Asia was similar.

For the next two decades cotton retained this extraordinarily favourable position in comparison to the other major agricultural products which continued to be subjected to 'non-equivalent exchange' through the imposition of compulsory delivery quotas at extremely low prices. For the 1930s and 1940s actual procurement prices for the agricultural goods are not available to us. Information about such prices is available from 1952 onwards and is summarised in Tables 2.13 and 2.14. In 1952 relative procurement prices of the major agricultural goods still retained the same general pattern as they did over the two preceding decades. Thus, an examination of the relative procurement prices in 1952 should give us a general impression of the relative advantage enjoyed by cotton during the period under review.

In 1952 the procurement price per ton of cotton was nearly 37 times that for grains. No estimates of relative costs of production in those days are available, but in recent years the average cost of production per ton of cotton was about seven times that for grain.[22] It is possible that, depending on whether techniques and relative input prices were different in the earlier period, the ratio of costs was different in those years. But such a difference could not have been very great. Thus net return per ton was many times higher for cotton than for grain. Indeed,

TABLE 2.13: Average Procurement Prices: (rubles per ton)

All USSR

	1952	1953	1955	1956	1958	1960	1962	1964	1965	1966	1967	1970	1975	1976
Grain Raw	8.67	20.5	47.9	55.0	60.3	62.2	72.3	72.3	89.7	98.2	103	97.2	111.8	96.0
Cotton	318.3	334.2	362.9	366.0	337.4	343.8	343.8	394.7	442.4	442.4	452.0	555.0	583.6	583.0
Meat	88.6	341.1	518.3	589.2	1041.1	1104.0	1353.8	1437.1	1589.7	1853.5	1873.6*	2278.0	2385.1	2441.4
Milk	29.1	58.8	88.2	97.2	117.6	117.6	126.9	133.0	148.5	153.9	156.0	191.9	215.1	217.0

Uzbekistan

	1952	1953	1955	1956	1958	1960	1962	1964	1965	1966	1967	1970	1975	1976
Grain Raw	–	–	–	–	–	–	–	–	157.8	–	–	157.0	172.2	150.6
Cotton	–	–	–	–	–	–	–	–	435.6	–	–	539.8	544.0	561.6

Tajikistan

	1952	1953	1955	1956	1958	1960	1962	1964	1965	1966	1967	1970	1972	1973
Grain Raw	–	–	–	–	–	63.5	–	–	99.5	–	–	144.4	126.5	148.8
Cotton	–	–	–	–	–	378.6	–	–	490.7	–	–	613.0	586.9	614.8

Source: The figures for 1965, 1970, 1975 and 1976 are calculated by dividing the payments by quantities shown in *NK SU 60, NK Uz. 60 and ST 50*. For 1967 the data are from V. R. Boev, *Zakupochnye Tseny i Chisty i, Dokhod Kolkhozov* Moscow 1969. For 1952 to 1967 indices are available in A. N. Malafeyev, *Istoriya Tsenoobrazovaniya v SSSR (1917–1963)*, Moscow 1964. Absolute prices have been found by applying these indices to the 1967 prices shown in Boev, op cit.

* The figure for 1967 in Boev, op cit is assumed to be the price for cattle in liveweight which we have converted to slaughterweight (liveweight = 1.56 times slaughterweight).

TABLE 2.14: A Comparison between Average Procurement Prices (all USSR) and International Prices: US Cents Per kilogramme (Current Price at Current Official Rate of Exchange)

Commodity	1952			1976		
	USSR Procurement Price (1)	International Price (2)	Ratio of (1) to (2)	USSR Procurement Price (1)	International Price (2)	Ratio of (1) to (2)
Grain	0.97	7.4	0.13	13.44	13.3	1.01
Meat	9.8	73.2	0.13	342	169	2.02
Cotton (lint equivalent)	104	79.4	1.31	233	176.0	1.32

International Prices: Grain: Simple average for wheat (US Hard Red Winter No. 2, *cif* North Sea Ports) and Corn (US Yellow No. 2/3 *cif* North Sea Ports).

Meat: For 1952: Beef, Steers, good, wholesale price Chicago. For 1976: unweighted average of export price from four countries shown in FAO *Production Yearbook* 1976.

Cotton: US Memphis 1 1/16" *cif* UK.

the net return on grain was negative and that on cotton highly positive.

Another way to look at the relative prices is to compare them with the prevailing international prices. Without implying that the prices in international trade were in some sense optimal one could argue that such a comparison shows the extent to which the state monopoly of external trade and the system of procurement have entailed asymmetrical degrees of income transfers from the producers of different agricultural products.

Such comparisons are, of course, extremely difficult. Since our main purpose is to look at the *relative* ratios of procurement prices to international prices we need not worry too much about the appropriateness of the official rate of exchange which has been used throughout. But the problem of the comparability of quality is a serious one and there is little doubt that the ratios shown in Table 2.14 contain significant elements of error due to this problem. Another point is that the procurement prices should properly be compared with the growers' prices elsewhere. Instead we have compared them with the wholesale or *cif* export prices in major producing or trading centres.

And yet the results are so strikingly different for different goods that one is not left in any doubt about the direction of bias in official policy. For grains and meat the average procurement price paid to the producers in the USSR in 1952 was less than one-seventh of the international price. For cotton the procurement price paid was nearly a third above the international price.[23] Thus relative to the production of other major agricultural goods (namely, grains and meat) the production of cotton was being subsidised (or taxed far less heavily).[24]

6. SOME CONSEQUENCES OF THE STRATEGY

(a) CHANGE IN CROPPING PATTERN

The main effects of the exceptionally favourable terms of trade for cotton need to be analysed in some detail. The first important effect to note is the sharp shift of sown area away from grain into cotton. In the pre-revolutionary days grain was the main crop in Central Asia both in terms of area and physical volume of production. In 1913 about 75 per cent of the sown land in Central Asia consisted of grain and only 15 per cent of cotton. By 1965 the share of grain had fallen to 41 per cent and that of cotton risen to 36 per cent. What is even more important to note is that most of the irrigated land came to be diverted to cotton while grain was gradually shifted to marginal and dry land. Thus, in quality units, the shift in area was far more dramatic than is indicated by the above figures. This is reflected in the relative outputs over time. Production of raw cotton and grains in Central Asia in 1913 and in 1961–5 (annual average) was as follows (thousand tons):

	1913	*1961–65 (annual average)*
Cotton	646	4466
Grains	1822	1756

In terms of physical weight grain fell from 2.82 times of cotton in 1913 to only 0.39 times in 1961–5. Between these time periods cotton production increased sevenfold while grain production declined in absolute terms.

This remarkable shift in cropping pattern was the result, not of coercion or administrative fiat, but of a systematic use of price incentives.[25] This constitutes an outstanding exception to the strategy of squeezing out surplus from agriculture that is usually attributed to the USSR.

The primary motivation behind this policy of favourable terms of trade for cotton was to ensure the quick achievement of national self-sufficiency in this basic commodity. This objective was achieved with singular success. The question remains whether this spectacular increase in specialisation in cotton was a movement in the direction of bringing into the open the potential comparative advantage (defined broadly to take into account the multiple social objectives and the limitations on trade possibilities) of the region in cotton or whether the specialisation went beyond the dictates of economic efficiency. To this very important question we shall return in Chapter 4.

(b) EMPLOYMENT

Table 2.15 shows that labour requirement per hectare is on the average six times higher for cotton than for grain in Kolkhoz in Uzbekistan. For Sovkhoz (which have generally a higher degree of mechanisation and a lower degree of labour-intensity as compared with Kolkhoz) the difference in labour requirement between cotton and grain is even greater. In the rest of Central Asia the orders of magnitude are roughly the same.

TABLE 2.15: Man-hours of Labour Required per Hectare of Cotton and Grain Cultivated in Uzbekistan: 1976

	Cotton	*Grain*	*Cotton as Multiple of Grain*
Kolkhoz	1089	181	6.02
Sovkhoz	666	58	11.48

Source: These calculations are based on the labour input per ton and output per hectare shown in *NK Uz. 60*.

Table 2.16 shows the trend in labour intensity over time. Labour requirement for grain cultivation has gone down quite dramatically over the last eleven years: in Uzbekistan it came down by more than 50 per cent while in the rest of the USSR

TABLE 2.16: Man-hours of Labour Required to Produce One Ton

		1965	*1970*	*1975*	*1976*
Uzbekistan					
Cotton:	Kolkhoz	380	370	350	330
	Sovkhoz	300	300	270	260
Grain:	Kolkhoz	155	96	124	74
	Sovkhoz	84	46	78	43
USSR					
Cotton:	Kolkhoz	400	370	360	350
	Sovkhoz	310	310	270	260
Grain:	Kolkhoz	47	19	19	14
	Sovkhoz	24	12	15	11

Source: *NK Uz. 60. NK SU 60*.

the decline was up to 70 per cent. In comparison, there has been a very slow reduction in the labour intensity of cotton cultivation. Over the corresponding period it came down by about 12 per cent in Uzbekistan and about 13 per cent in the rest of Central Asia. Thus the gap in the labour requirement between cotton and the other crops has been increasing over time.[26]

It may be a little inappropriate to compare the average labour requirement in cotton and grain. As we have already observed, grain is usually cultivated on un-irrigated or less irrigated land. Such cultivation is less intensive. Thus, if some of the irrigated cotton land were to be converted into grain land, the labour requirement in grain at the margin would probably be somewhat higher than it is now on the average. But it is clear that this would still be only a fraction of that for cotton.

We, therefore, arrive at the important finding that the increased specialisation in cotton led to a much greater demand for labour in agriculture in Central Asia than would have been the case otherwise. This is probably one of the most important factors contributing to the lower rate of urbanisation for the Central Asian republics over the recent decades. Cotton cultivation continued to absorb such a high proportion of the labour force that in spite of its rapid rate of growth the proportion deployable in the non-agricultural sectors increased slowly.

(c) DIFFERENCE IN SECTORAL INCOMES

To make increased demand for labour effective, it was necessary to offer them a high enough income that would induce them to stay on the farm. It is here that the favourable terms of trade for cotton played a crucial role. After the mid-1930s agricultural incomes grew very fast and the income payments, especially to the Kolkhoz workers, were high enough to render the pull of the wages offered by the urban industries relatively weak.

We do not have information about the differences in sectoral wages in the earlier years but Table 2.17 summarises some information for 1965 and 1975. As we have already

TABLE 2.17: A Comparison Between Incomes in Industry, Kolkhoz and
State Agriculture: 1965 and 1975

	Industry ÷ Kolkhoz		State Agriculture ÷ Kolkhoz		Industry ÷ State Agriculture	
	1965	1975	1965	1975	1965	1975
USSR	1.56	1.43	1.12	1.12	1.39	1.28
Uzbekistan	1.14	1.32	0.84	1.05	1.36	1.26
Tajikistan	1.16	1.19	0.93	0.87	1.25	1.36

Note: For industry and State agriculture monthly wages have been used. For
Kolkhoz payment per man-day has been multiplied by 25. In reality a Kolkhoz
worker works for less than 25 days a month but this number has been used due
to the fact that in industry a worker works for about 25 days a month. For State
agriculture (mainly Sovkhoz) the monthly payment is presumably also
standardised for a full month of approximately 25 days. The sources are the
same as for the data in table 2·8.

noted, the difference between Central Asia and the rest of the
USSR in terms of agricultural income had already narrowed
substantially by 1965. And yet it is revealing that the difference
in earnings between urban industries and rural Kolkhoz was so
much lower in Central Asia than in the rest of the USSR, even
at as recent a date as 1965.

It should be recognised that the comparison between
earnings from collective labour gives an incomplete picture of
the comparative living standards. Further allowances must be
made for a number of additional factors. First, one should
allow for the payments out of public consumption fund for
which the available all-Union data show that the payment for
an urban worker's family was 37 per cent higher than that for
the family of a Kolkhoznik in 1965.[27] No such information is
available for the Central Asian republics separately. There is,
however, no particular reason to suppose that the relation-
ship there is very different from what it is at the all-Union
level.

Next, one must allow for the income from private sources,
notably from the personal auxiliary plots. Income from this
source is much less for the urban workers (who, contrary to

usual expectation also frequently have personal plots) than for the Kolkhozniki. What is important to note is that this source of income is a much lower proportion of income in Central Asia than elsewhere.[28] Thus, this factor would exert a smaller equalising influence between urban-rural income differential in Central Asia than in the USSR as a whole.

The other factors for which allowances should be made are the difference in the dependency ratio and the difference in cost of living. On these we have no useful information to base any guess upon. Urban families are probably smaller. On cost of living it is very difficult to judge which sector has the advantage.

The total effect of these factors would almost certainly be to reduce the industry-Kolkhoz income differential at the all-Union level. For the Central Asian republics the results would probably be similar except that the extent of such reduction may be somewhat smaller. It, however, appears that even after all these adjustments the industry-Kolkhoz differential for 1965 would remain higher for all USSR than for Central Asia.

It is highly likely that the differential was relatively even lower for Central Asia in the earlier years. If one takes the trends in Tables 2.8 and 2.9 to be accurate and extrapolates them backwards to the 1950s, one would conclude that the sectoral income differential in those years was in favour of Kolkhoz in Central Asia.

Another important fact that stands out from the data in Table 2.17 is the asymmetrical relation between earnings in state agriculture (mainly Sovkhoz) and Kolkhoz in the USSR as a whole and Central Asia. In the USSR as a whole Sovkhoz earnings are significantly higher than Kolkhoz earnings. Public policy has the stated objective of equalising the earnings from the two sources. In the Central Asian republics such differentials have been much less. Indeed, in 1965 the payments in Kolkhoz were greater than those in state agriculture. Even in 1975 that remains true for Tajikistan while for Uzbekistan the ratio alters moderately in favour of state agriculture. This fact probably explains part of the phenomenon of the relatively slow growth of the Sovkhoz in Central Asia.

7. CHANGES SINCE 1953

Beginning 1953 the policy of extremely low procurement prices for the agricultural goods began to change. Over the next decade the prices of grains, meat and milk were increased steadily and rapidly and the rise in the prices of the livestock products continued at a rapid rate to date (see Table 2.13). By 1962 grain price had risen more than eight-fold over the 1952 level. The procurement prices for meat and milk increased by more than 15 and 4 times respectively over the same period. During this period of spectacular rise in the prices of other goods the procurement price of cotton remained virtually unchanged.[29]

By 1962 per ton procurement price was only 4.76 times higher for cotton than for grains. The cost of production per ton of cotton is 7.42 times that of grains for the USSR as a whole. Thus the price to cost ratio had altered sharply in favour of grains.[30]

As a result of the sharply lowered relative incentive for cotton its production and yield ceased to grow as rapidly as in the earlier decades. In many areas production and yield fell between the early 1950s and early 1960s. The effect on peasant income was much more severe. During these years the Sovkhoz specialising in cotton were making substantial losses.[31] It has also been claimed that incomes at the Uzbek collective farms declined by 17 per cent between the years 1957 and 1960.[32]

After unsuccessfully trying out various administrative methods of persuading the cotton growers to produce more, the procurement price was increased substantially in 1963 after a long period of stagnation. Thereafter prices were increased in a number of further steps and such increases have generally been at a higher rate than that for grains, the main competing crop. By 1976 some of the relative price advantage lost over the period 1953–62 was restored. Especially in the Central Asian republics the relative procurement prices of cotton and grain were carefully balanced to keep the price-cost ratio higher for cotton.[33] Thus, according to the data shown in Table 2.13, the ratios of procurement prices of cotton and grains in 1976 were

3.73 and 4.13 respectively for Uzbekistan and Tajikistan. The ratios of costs of production at Kolkhoz were respectively 3.53 and 3.62.[34]

Table 2.14 shows the comparison between procurement prices and the prices in the international market in 1976 at the official rate of exchange. As compared to the pre-1953 years the position of grains has improved dramatically. While in 1952 these were paid only 13 per cent of the international price in 1976 these received a little more than the price in the world market. The position of cotton remains the same as in 1952. Thus cotton still received a higher protection (or was subjected to a lower rate or concealed taxation depending on how different the appropriate rate of exchange was from the official one) as compared to the grains.[35] The really dramatic change occurred for meat. By 1976 it had become a very heavily protected item; its procurement price was more than twice as high as that in the world market.

But, clearly, cotton had lost once and for all the extraordinarily privileged position it had until 1953. This is reflected in the comparatively slower rate of expansion in cotton production in the recent decades. Unfortunately, we do not have the necessary data to calculate the growth rates separately since 1953. The middle time period in Table 2.18 shows the average of the rates for two dissimilar periods, the years before 1953 and the years since. And yet it is clear that in both Uzbekistan and Tajikistan the rates of growth of cotton production have been declining steadily through the successive time periods. In Uzbekistan the growth rate in the output of grain has been substantial over the last decade—nearly twice as high as for cotton—as compared to the negative or negligible rates of growth in the preceding four decades. In both the republics livestock products have been growing much faster than in the earlier periods and, indeed, much more rapidly than cotton.

Although the gap between agricultural income in Central Asia and in the rest of the USSR has been narrowing, there has been a steady growth in agricultural income payments in Central Asia during the last decade. Table 2.8 shows the trends in payments per man-day in Kolkhoz. In Uzbekistan there was an increase of 51 per cent in eleven years leading to

TABLE 2.18: Annual Compound Rates of Growth of Major Agricultural Products (%)

Uzbekistan

	Between 1924 and 1940	Between 1940 and 1965	Between 1965 and 1975
Meat	3.5	2.8	5.1
Milk	3.5	2.9	6.4
Grain	−1.5	0.2	5.6
Cotton	12.7	4.1	3.0

Tajikistan

	Between 1929 and 1940	Between 1940 and 1965	Between 1965 and 1973
Meat	0.0	2.2	4.6
Milk	1.5	2.2	5.3
Grain	–	–	–
Cotton	12.5	5.2	3.2*

* Between 1965 and 1976
Source: *NK SU 60. NK Uz. 60. ST 50.*

1976 – an annual compound rate of 3.8 per cent. In Tajikistan the increase was 36 per cent in eight years leading to 1973 – an annual compound rate of 3.9 per cent. The increase in monthly payments to the employees in the state agricultural enterprises was also very impressive over the corresponding periods in Uzbekistan and Tajikistan – respectively 5.7 per cent and 3.1 per cent compounded annually.

These rates of growth refer to payments valued at current prices, however. To determine the real rate of growth it is necessary to deflate them by indices of costs of living. Unfortunately, no comprehensive index of cost of living is available for this purpose. Table 2.19 summarises the available price information.[36] The price index for state retail trade was absolutely stable over the 1965–76 period; there was a slight increase in the price of food which was more than offset by a decline in the price of non-food items.

It is, however, well-known that a good deal of consumption goods is purchased from non-state retail outlets such as the

TABLE 2.19: Price Indices

Year	State Retail Trade					Urban Kolkhoz Market (excluding Cattle)
	All Goods	Food			Non-food	
		All Food	Food without Alcoholic Drinks	Alcoholic Drinks		
1940	100	100	100	100	100	100
1950	186	203	187	289	165	98
1952	161	166	–	–	156	–
1953	146	146	–	–	145	–
1955	138	141	–	–	134	112
1960	139	147	–	–	130	108
1965	140	152	133	258	126	127
1968	139	151	–	–	124	137
1970	139	152	133	262	124	–
1975	139	154	133	267	122	–
1976	139	154	133	267	122	–

Source: *NK SU 60* and previous issues quoted in Roger Clarke, *Soviet Economic Facts, 1917–1970.*

Kolkhoz markets. We have no information about the index of the prices of goods purchased from such outlets. Nor do we know the magnitude of such purchase in the budget of an average peasant. But there are strong reasons to suggest that the price index of the sale through such outlets may not at all be correlated with that for the sales through the state retail trade.

Table 2.19 also shows the price index for sales at the urban Kolkhoz markets for the period up to 1968 (when its publication was discontinued). Since prices at such markets are determined by the free market forces they are far more volatile than the prices at the State retail enterprises. More important, this index shows an upward trend over much of the period since 1950 (with some notable deviations on either side of the trend) which is not at all in agreement with the movement in the price index of state sales. The trend rate of growth over the period from 1950 to 1968 was 2.3 per cent per year.[37] During the three years after 1965 prices increased at these Kolkhoz markets at an annual rate of about 2.5 per cent. There are 17 sets of observations (not all of them shown in table 2.19 for price index for food at State retail trade and the price index at the urban Kolkhoz markets. These observations show no correlation between the price changes at the State shops and the Kolkhoz markets.[38]

It is, therefore, probable that the prices at the non-state outlets have not been as stable as those at the state outlets. But, if the evidence of the index for the urban Kolkhoz markets is anything to go by, the rise in such prices has been modest. If we take the trend rate of growth of the urban Kolkhoz market prices for the period 1950–68 and (arbitrarily) assume that 40 per cent of consumer expenditure was directed at the non-state outlets (which is undoubtedly an exaggeration) the annual rate of increase in cost of living would work out to be as low as 0.9 per cent per year.

The above analysis indicates that the rise in agricultural earnings in Central Asia over the last decade has been fairly high in real terms. Earnings in Kolkhoz have been increasing at an annual average rate of nearly four per cent as compared to an annual increase in cost of living of no more than one per cent. It should, however, be recognised that the estimates of the increases in cost of living underlying this conclusion are based on too many arbitrary assumptions to warrant confidence.

An interesting point to note is that the state retail sale prices for agricultural goods declined since 1952. Over this period state payments for procurement increased at a spectacular rate. Thus profits from state trading in agricultural goods, a major source of state revenue in the earlier years, must by the mid-1970s have become large negative items for the USSR state budget. Published budget data do not allow a proper analysis of the question. Our crude estimates suggest that in 1976 the state payment for agricultural procurement was nearly 33 billion rubles more than what it would be had the procurement prices been unchanged at the 1952 level.[39] Thus as a consequence of the steady and sharp improvement allowed in the terms of trade for agriculture over the period since 1953 the state has forgone a potential revenue of 33 billion rubles per year by 1976. In 1976 this amount was $8\frac{1}{2}$ per cent of national income, 14 per cent of all state revenue and over 31 per cent of all capital accumulation. It is obvious that the improved terms of trade for agriculture were financed by a massive restructuring of the sources of state revenue and capital accumulation.

3 The Evolution and Working of Collective Farms

In this chapter we first provide a brief description of the evolution of collective agriculture in the Soviet Central Asian region and of the major landmarks which characterised this process. This is followed by an analysis of some aspects of the working of collective farms, and in particular of the autonomy enjoyed by a collective farm as a productive enterprise. There is also a discussion of the organisation and management of collective farms. We conclude the chapter with some tentative ideas on participation and decision-making in a Kolkhoz.

1. THE PROCESS OF COLLECTIVISATION IN SOVIET CENTRAL ASIA

The first major task after the October Revolution was to redistribute the land hitherto concentrated in the hands of the *bais* (feudal landowners) among the *dekhans* (peasants). The beginning was made, immediately after the establishment of Soviet power in Central Asia, by the nationalisation of land and water. The first land and water reform took place in 1921–2. Through this step significant advance was made in the direction of redistribution in favour of poorer peasants who received free land for their use. But this reform left the bigger landowners unexpropriated so that a good deal of social stratification continued to exist in the agricultural sector of the region. Thus the social composition of the landowners and peasants in Uzbekistan during the middle of the 1920s was described as consisting of 'landowners who did not work or

only partly worked in their households; landowners who lived
in town permanently and rented out their land; owners of
allotments (middle and poor peasants); landless peasants, and
others'.[1]

A number of important points need to be noted. In
Uzbekistan in 1925 about 41 per cent of the peasant households rented in land on a cropsharing basis and, on the
average, such rented land amounted to two-thirds of their total
holdings.[2] Landlessness was prevalent on a significant scale.
Urban merchants, thriving under the New Economic Policy,
owned rural land that was rented out.

The second land-and-water reform was introduced during
the period 1925–28 to abolish these exploitative institutions. A
land fund for distribution among the landless and the poor
peasants was set up by confiscating the land of the households
whose members did not work and by adding to it the newly
irrigated state and communal land. Big feudal-bai landownership and the absentee-ownership by the urban merchants were
completely abolished. As a result of redistribution the pattern
of landownership became much more equal.[3] A survey of
11,700 households which were allotted land in Uzbekistan
showed that the proportion of sharecroppers declined from 41
per cent to 6 per cent and that, for the sharecroppers, the ratio
of rented land to total landholding declined from 67 per cent to
an insignificant 0.03 per cent.[4] For all practical purposes land
renting was rendered an insignificant practice after the reform.
During the reform a beginning was made to set up collective
and state farms on state land and land expropriated from
landlords. But these collective farms were small and in-
sufficiently endowed with capital assets. By 1928 not much
more than 1 per cent of the rural households in Central Asia
were organised in the collective forms of agriculture.

The pace of collectivisation was accelerated in Central Asia
at about the same time as in the rest of the USSR. The account
is well known and hardly needs to be retold. The Soviet
leadership was deeply worried by the failure of the procurement targets of 1928. To them this was an act of sabotage by
the Kulaks who were still powerful in the rural USSR. The
issue had become particularly crucial in view of the launching
of the First Five-Year Plan in May 1929. The success of the

plan depended on the generation of an adequate marketable surplus of food and agricultural raw materials. The leadership became convinced that the only way to ensure these objectives was to liquidate the Kulaks and organise the peasantry into collective farms. The pace of collectivisation was accordingly speeded up suddenly in the last quarter of 1929 to reach massive proportions.[5]

Table 3.1 shows that the pace of collectivisation in Central Asia was not in any way slower than that in the rest of the USSR. Indeed, from a somewhat lower start in 1928, the most important Central Asian republic overtook the USSR as a whole in terms of the percentage of rural households in collective agriculture within the first year of the intensification of the campaign. Available accounts suggest that resistance to collectivisation was quite strong on the part of the nomadic population (the 'Kulak' elements among them) specialising in livestock production. But resistance in those areas of Central Asia where settled agriculture had been in practice was probably less intense than that experienced elsewhere in the USSR.

TABLE 3.1: Percentage of Rural Households in Collective Agriculture

Year	Uzbekistan	Tajikistan	Turkmenistan	Kirghizia	USSR
1928	1.2	0.2	1.7	0.5	1.7
1929	3.0	–	–	–	–
1930	34.4	–	–	–	23.6
1931	68.2	–	–	–	61.5
1932	81.7	–	–	–	–
1937	95.0	–	–	–	93.0
1938	97.6	–	–	–	–
1940	99.8	98.7	98.9	99.4	96.9

Note: The figures refer to the membership in all kinds of collective organisations, Kolkhoz and Sovkhoz included. The Uzbek data are from *NK Uz. 60* and the rest from *NKSU 60*.

2. THE EVOLUTION OF THE COLLECTIVE FARMS

In this section we shall present a brief account of the major landmarks in the evolution of collective agriculture. These organisational measures applied more or less uniformly throughout the USSR. We shall, therefore, discuss some of the all-Union measures that applied equally to Central Asia.

During the process of collectivisation in the USSR various organisational forms of collective agriculture were tried. Once the process of bringing the rural households within the fold of collective organisation was completed it was, therefore, necessary to introduce a uniform set of practices to guide the operations of the collectives. This was the objective of the Model Rules of the Collective Farm adopted by the Second All-Union Congress of Collective Farmers held in 1935. The main provisions of the Model Rules, some of which were subsequently incorporated in the Constitution of the USSR, may be summarised as follows.

Land was declared the property of all people but its use was secured to the *artel*[6] for ever free of rent. The artels could not buy, sell or let land. Means of production, e.g., draught animals, agricultural implements (ploughs, sowers, harrows, threshers, mowers, etc.), seed reserve, forage for collectively owned livestock and buildings needed for collective farming, would be owned collectively.

An important fact about capital equipment that needs to be noted is that the collective farms were not vested with the ownership of modern machinery like tractors and harvesters. These were vested in the Machine Tractor Stations (MTS) which were state organisations financed by state budget. Each MTS served a number of collective farms who had to enter into annual agreements with MTS for the performance of the operations that required the services of such machines. Thus, the MTS served as a very effective organ of control in the implementation of the production plans in agriculture.

The artels were authorised to allocate personal plots of land to the member households. Such plots could vary between one quarter to one half of a hectare in size although in certain districts the upper limit could be as high as one hectare. Personal dwellings, personal cattle, poultry, buildings necessary to keep personal cattle and minor farm implements were not pooled into collective ownership. A limited amount of services of collectively owned capital (e.g., draught animals) could be made available on payment for use on personal plots.

The limit on the personal ownership of livestock varied from one region to another. In the crop growing areas such limit consisted of one cow, two calves, one or two sows with sucklings, 10 sheep and goats taken together, unlimited poultry and rabbits and 20 beehives. In the non-nomadic or semi-nomadic stockbreeding regions (in which fell much of Central Asia) the limits were much higher—four or five cows with their calves, 30 or 40 sheep and goats taken together, two or three sows with sucklings, an unlimited number of poultry and rabbits and 20 beehives. In the nomadic stockbreeding regions the limits on the personal ownership of livestock were about twice as high as in the non-nomadic regions.

All toilers of the age of 16 or more could become members of a collective subject to the approval by the General Meeting. There was a membership fee of 20 to 40 rubles.

The labour input into the activities of the collective farms was to be provided by the member households. Non-members could be employed only if they were people possessing special qualifications (agronomists, engineers, etc.).

The General Meeting of all members was to be the highest administrative authority within a collective farm. It elected the Chairman and the members of the Board of Management which administered the day to day affairs of the collective. It admitted new members and decided on questions of resignation and expulsion of members. It approved production plans and revenue and expenditure budgets. It authorised contracts with the MTS.

A collective farm was to consist of a number of brigades. Members of field brigades in cropping operations were to be assigned for a full period of crop rotation. Members of stockbreeding brigades were to be assigned for a period of not less than three years. Work in the brigade will be assigned by the brigadier who will be elected by the members. All agricultural operations would be performed on the basis of piece-work remuneration. Rates of remuneration would be fixed for each separate job in terms of labour days. Brigades which exceed (fall short of) the average performance for the artel were to receive an increase (reduction) in the remuneration of all members by up to 10 per cent of their total labour days.

The next major landmark in the evolution of the collective farms was the large scale merger and amalgamation that took place in the early 1950s. In a sense some amount of merger to promote an average increase in size has been taking place since the 1930s and continuing to the present day. But in the early 1950s the process was sharply accelerated. Table 3.2 shows the trends for Tajikistan. Unfortunately, we do not have the estimates for the years in the early 1950s, but it is known that much of the dramatic change in size revealed by the comparison between the data for 1940 and 1960 did take place in those years.

TABLE 3.2: Changes in the Size of Kolkhoz in Tajikistan

	1940	*1960*	*1965*	*1973*
Number of Kolkhoz	3093	353	309	251
Number of Kolkhoz households (thousand)	196.9	198.8	230.7	216.1
Number of households per Kolkhoz	64	563	747	861
Hectares of sown land per Kolkhoz	248	1779	2045	1949

Source: *ST 50*.

As a result of the merger the average size of a collective farm increased dramatically. Of greater importance is the fact that as a consequence of merger the average size of a brigade went up. In many cases a former Kolkhoz became a brigade of a bigger Kolkhoz that was created by a merger of a number of smaller ones. Even after the amalgamation and the continued increase in size to the present day an average Kolkhoz in Uzbekistan had 866 and that in Tajikistan had 861 member households in 1976. These are about twice as large as the average for the USSR as a whole which, in 1976, was 486.

The process of merger has not been uniform. In some cases several Kolkhozy were amalgamated to form a new one. In other cases Kolkhozy were merged with a Sovkhoz or were merged together to form a new Sovkhoz. This latter phenomenon of converting a Kolkhoz into a Sovkhoz has continued, probably at an accelerating rate, up till the present.

Table 3.3 shows the trends in the USSR, Uzbekistan and Tajikistan over the last decade. Because of a lower initial level the proportion of labour force in Sovkhoz remains lower in Central Asia than in the rest of the USSR. The trend, however, is the same as that for the Union as a whole.

The justification for this phenomenon has consisted of the argument that many Kolkhozy have persisted being un-economic, so they had to be taken into the fold of the Sovkhoz structure. The implied argument is either that the state-bureaucratic management is more efficient than some degree of self-management, or that the state management and ownership permits an easier injection of resources into these units from outside.

The next major landmark in the evolution of collective agriculture was the abolition of the Machine Tractor Stations (MTS) in 1958. Henceforward, the collective farms were to own machines and tractors whose services they previously hired from the MTS.

Unfortunately, the process of the liquidation of the MTS is inadequately documented. It is not known to what extent the collectives were allowed to select the machines that they bought, given credit to finance purchase and given discounts on the second-hand equipment. It has, however, been sugges-ted that the increased flexibility and decentralisation permitted by the abolition of the MTS were not without cost. Thus, the average area ploughed by a tractor is reported to have declined by 21 per cent between 1960 and 1964.[7] Once again, it is unclear if this were due to the lack of skill and efficiency within the collectives or the greater difficulty on the part of the collective farms, as compared to the state-run MTS, to obtain spares which were perpetually short in supply.

Over the three and a half decades since the adoption of the Model Rules in 1935 the structure of collective agriculture underwent many changes of which some have been outlined above. To formalise all these changes the Third All-Union Congress of Kolkhoz members adopted a new Model Charter in 1969. The rules governing the operation and organisation of collective farms are discussed below in more detail. Here we give a brief account of the major points of difference between the new charter and that of 1935.

TABLE 3.3: Number of Kolkhoz and Sovkhoz Workers

	All USSR (Million Workers)			Uzbekistan (Thousand Workers)			Tajikistan (Thousand Workers)		
	Kolkhoz	*Sovkhoz*	*Sovkhoz as % of Total*	*Kolkhoz*	*Sovkhoz*	*Sovkhoz as % of Total*	*Kolkhoz*	*Sovkhoz*	*Sovkhoz as % of Total*
1965	18.6	8.2	31	971.7	343.3	26	285	29.8	9
1970	16.7	8.9	35	1029.4	392.2	28	263	59.1	18
1975	15.2	10.3	40	1046.6	572.9	35	258*	80.2*	24*
1976	14.8	11.0	43	1045.8	607.9	37	–	–	–

* The figures are for 1973
Source: *NK SU 60. NK Uz 60. ST 50.*

To the list of communal property were added tractors, combines and other machines and Kolkhoz shares of the assets of the inter-Kolkhoz and state-Kolkhoz enterprises.

Hiring of specialist labour from outside continued to be permitted. Besides piece-rate working provisions for job-rate payment, time-rate and other systems of payment were incorporated. Provision for guaranteed minimum pay for all collective farm members was introduced. Generally more comprehensive provisions for social security were spelled out.

Regulations concerning 'personal auxiliary farming' by the members of the collective farms were left roughly unchanged. Personal plots could be up to 0.2 hectare if irrigated and 0.5 hectare if unirrigated. Dwelling houses, farm buildings, small implements, animal sheds, one cow with one calf up to two years, one heifer or bull up to two years, one sow with pigs up to three months or two hogs being fattened, up to 10 sheep and goats and beehives, poultry and rabbits could all be personally owned by each household. Personal plots could also be awarded to non-members (e.g., teachers, office employees and workers) living within the Kolkhoz territory, subject to the availability of land.

The main change about the rules of management consisted of the substitution of Representatives Meeting for General Meeting in the case of the larger collective farms. Such representatives would be elected by the brigades and other units. Another feature of the new charter was the vastly increased importance of the specialists appointed by the board

> to guide individual branches of the collective farm's activity . . . The instructions of chief (senior) specialists on questions falling within their purview are mandatory for collective farm members and also for the officials of the collective farm.[8]

3. WORKING OF THE KOLKHOZ

(a) THE EXTERNAL FRAMEWORK

The Model Collective Farm Charter adopted in 1969 defines a Kolkhoz as 'a co-operative organisation of voluntarily associated peasants for the joint conduct of large-scale agricultural production on the basis of communal means of production and collective labour'. As a voluntary, co-operative association of producers in a planned, socialist economy, the Kolkhoz presents some interesting and distinctive features. It differs from state enterprises which are the more usual form of organisation in a socialist economy not only in the ownership pattern of means of production but, perhaps more importantly, in the greater autonomy it enjoys in principle both in production and management. By the same token, in principle, the Kolkhoz provides greater scope for participation and democratic decision-making than may be possible in a state enterprise which comes directly under a ministry and is, therefore, more liable to political and bureaucratic control. At the same time, however, the Kolkhozy operate within the framework of a centrally planned economy which must, by its sheer logic, provide for the regulations of their activities. This is so for two main reasons. Firstly, the Kolkhozy are important producers of food and raw materials and their contribution must be fitted into the planned supply and demand of these commodities. Secondly, the incomes and standard of living of the Kolkhozniki are matters of national concern as part of the overall policy on income distribution and material welfare. These two considerations alone would necessitate the creation of a mechanism to influence the activities of the Kolkhozy in appropriate directions. The autonomy enjoyed by the Kolkhozy is thus circumscribed by the dictates of central planning and considerations of national policy. But the extent to which it is so and the mechanisms and instruments devised for this end bear directly on participation and organisation within a Kolkhoz. We look, therefore, first at the changing framework governing the activities of the Kolkhozy, before turning to a discussion of their organisation and operation.

The external framework within which a Kolkhoz must conduct its activities comprises not only the macroeconomic factors mentioned above but also a whole host of laws, institutions and practices operating at the national, regional and local levels. These include, for example, the role of the Communist Party both in providing overall policy guidelines and in promoting their implementation at the level of the individual Kolkhoz; the myriad state bodies to which the Kolkhoz must relate on a vast variety of subjects; and a complex corpus of legislation defining rights, obligations and liabilities of the Kolkhozy and their members. It is beyond the scope of this monograph to delve into these matters. Our discussion in this section is limited to assessing the degree of autonomy enjoyed by the Kolkhoz in its role as a productive enterprise. As such, we are concerned primarily with the determination of the quantities and prices of the outputs and inputs of a Kolkhoz.

The first issue concerns the amount, composition and pricing of the output of a Kolkhoz. The price of the commodities sold to the state procurement agencies is fixed in advance by the state. Under the present system, there is a single procurement price for some products, but for several important commodities such as cotton, grains and meat, there is a two-layer pricing arrangement: a basic quota price and a premium price—generally 50 per cent above the basic price— for above quota deliveries to the state. Surplus produce from collective farms as well as personal plots may also be sold in Kolkhoz markets where the price is determined by the forces of supply and demand.

The more significant question concerns the determination of the Kolkhoz output. A distinctive feature of the Soviet system is that individual Kolkhozy enter into long-term contracts with state agencies to supply specified amounts of agricultural produce. The key issue, therefore, is the determination of the quota for an individual Kolkhoz. The quotas are fixed by the state bodies after consultation with the Kolkhozy. Some of the factors that are taken into account in determining quotas are past performance, present capacity (based on availability of land, capital and labour), future needs and planned expansion of capacity. This is an inherently difficult exercise, and even with the use of 'the most scientific methods' it is inevitable that quotas for individual farms should show considerable divergence in relation to their 'normal productive capacity'. The quotas serve as constraints on the production plan and, to a large extent, limit the possibility of its variation. The quotas, however, represent minimum output and it is still open to the individual Kolkhoz to decide on the amount and composition of output it wishes to produce after meeting quota requirements. The degree of flexibility it has in this respect will naturally depend on the ratio of quotas to its 'productive capacity'. It should also be noted that the existence of personal plots and livestock provides another element of output flexibility to the Kolkhoznik, if not to the Kolkhoz as a collective enterprise. Subject to the limitations imposed by resource availability, a Kolkhoznik is free to produce what he likes on his personal plot and to sell it in the market of his choice.

Given the output quotas, the autonomy enjoyed by the Kolkhoz as a productive enterprise depends in large measure on the flexibility it has with respect to factor availability and utilisation. Here the position has changed quite considerably since the early 1950s. Prior to that, not only had the state organs greater say in fixing quotas, but they also exercised extensive and direct control over the Kolkhozy to ensure that the plan targets were met. This control was exercised through such means as the specification of the amount of land to be allocated to individual crops and the application of other inputs in physical terms, the leasing of machinery and equipment from the Machine Tractor Stations (which also supplied various kinds of technical and skilled services to the farms) and the regulations pertaining to the proportion of revenue to be allocated to overall investment and to individual items. In all these respects, the independence enjoyed by the Kolkhozy has improved a good deal since the early 1950s. For instance, a decree in March 1955 foreshadowed a shift from the external specification of detailed plan targets for such variables as sown area, deliveries etc., to a system under which 'collective farms were to receive a delivery plan, and the farms themselves would work out a plan specifying changes in sown area and cattle herds as necessary for the fulfilment of the delivery targets'.[9] In 1965 there was a shift from annual to five year procurement targets which must be considered a major contribution to the enhanced autonomy of the Kolkhozy. The Machine Tractor Stations were abolished in 1958 and their equipment and many of the skilled personnel were transferred to the Kolkhozy, thus increasing their control over the utilisation of two crucial inputs. A similar move to greater economic independence for the Kolkhozy was signalled by the formal abolition of investment ratios to be applied to the Kolkhoz revenue and their easier access to credit from the banks.[10]

What is then the current position with respect to input availability and use? The main inputs to consider are land, capital, labour and knowledge. *Land* is made available to the Kolkhoz by the state on a rent-free basis for perpetuity. Although a Kolkhoz is allocated a fixed amount of land, the sown area is generally considerably less than the total arable land. Thus the Kolkhoz can increase the effective size of the cultivated area by bringing some of the existing arable land under cultivation, extending irrigation or by altering the fallow system. Another avenue open to the Kolkhoz and one which as shown earlier has been promoted by the state and extensively used in the 1950s and 1960s is amalgamation with contiguous farms. Finally, the Kolkhoz can apply for an increase in the arable land available to it. In most parts of the Central Asian Republics it is not so much the availability of land *per se* which is the crucial factor but, given the soil and the climatic factors, it is the access to irrigated land which determines productive potential. Thus the land frontier of the Kolkhoz in this case can only be extended by massive investment in land improvement which is usually beyond the ability of a single collective to mobilise.

Capital is represented not only by buildings, machinery and equipment etc., but also by such items as roads, electrification, irrigation and other land-improvement schemes. The responsibility for the accumulation of such capital is shared between the Kolkhozy and the state. The state is responsible for constructing and financing large-scale irrigation, water works, electrification, roads, etc., while minor projects in these areas as well as acquisition of machinery, equipment, fertilizers, etc., are financed by the Kolkhoz. These have to be financed essentially out of internal savings or through long-term borrowing from the financial sector. As indicated earlier, the ability of the Kolkhoz to determine the volume and pattern of own investment has been considerably enhanced in recent years. The role of the state in agricultural investment undertaken in the Kolkhozy nevertheless remains considerable. This consists not only in supplying the Kolkhoz with norms and recommendations on investment policy but more importantly in determining the price and output of capital goods. Furthermore, as indicated above, a significant proportion of infrastructural investment is undertaken and financed by the state organs.

Next we consider *labour* availability to the Kolkhoz. The main source of labour supply to the Kolkhoz is the working time of its members. The Kolkhoz can augment its labour supply by taking on new members (an unimportant source in practice) and by recruiting workers for short periods. But it is the amount of time put in by the members and their families which in practice provides flexibility in labour supply to the Kolkhoz. This flexibility is needed especially at times of peak agricultural activity such as sowing, weeding and above all harvesting. During these periods, the Kolkhoz can and does draw upon its 'hidden reserves of labour' as represented, for example, by the diversion to agriculture of the working time of women and students.

A second source of flexibility is provided by the division of the members' time between work on the collective and the personal plots. The labour requirements of meeting delivery targets represent minimum needs for collective work. The additional labour that the Kolkhoz can attract into a collective plot will depend on the relative remuneration in personal and collective farming and the labour needs on the personal plot which in turn are determined by the size of the plot and the technology in use. It is general practice by the Kolkhozy to stipulate the minimum required numbers of work days for collective activities.

Thus the pattern and rate of supply of labour of its members in a Kolkhoz depend, at any given structure of rewards, on the members preference for leisure and work on personal plots. The state does not seem to play any direct role in determining labour supply and allocation at the Kolkhoz. However, the role of the state in influencing the pattern and rate of remuneration is quite considerable and has changed over time.[11] Rules for the payment of collective farm leadership personnel (base and supplementary pay) were set forth in a decree of April 1948. These were modified by the decree of

March 1956 passed by the Central Committee of the CPSU which recommended that Kolkhozy themselves, in accordance with local conditions, establish the supplementary payment for leadership personnel. In the early 1960s several steps were taken to promote greater uniformity in incentive schemes, which on balance must have led to greater centralisation. For all Kolkhoz members, the major change came in 1966 when a guaranteed minimum wage was effectively established in place of the earlier system under which the remuneration of a Kolkhoznik depended on the residual after all other expenses had been met. The state has since followed a policy of progressively ensuring uniformity in remuneration and social welfare benefits for workers in the Kolkhozy and the state enterprises. Its net effect has been to reduce the autonomy of the Kolkhozy in determining the remuneration and social welfare benefits for its members. This has, however, been counterbalanced to some extent by their greater independence in determining payment and bonus schemes.

The *knowledge* factor refers to skilled personnel and diffusion of the results of research and development (R and D). In this regard, there has been a clear gain over the past two decades in terms of the autonomy enjoyed by the Kolkhozy. As far as skilled personnel are concerned, the increase in autonomy has been the result primarily of three factors. Firstly, from 1955 onwards there was a steady transfer of skilled personnel from the MTSs, to the Kolkhozy, a trend which was intensified after the abolition of MTSs in 1958. Secondly, in an attempt to boost their managerial ability, the government initiated a large-scale recruitment of top officials for the Kolkhozy from the cities. The '20,000 ers'—as they were called in the 1955 campaign—while contributing to an upliftment of the managerial capabilities of the Kolkhozy must have seriously diluted the control over policy exercised by the Kolkhozniks. There has been no repetition of external recruitment on this scale in the subsequent years. In our visits to the collective farms in the two Central Asian Republics, it seemed clear that the great majority of persons holding managerial and specialist posts had been recruited from within rather than from outside.

The third factor has been the enormous expansion of

secondary, technical and vocational education in the post-war period. This has naturally resulted in a great improvement in the educational and technical qualifications of the Kolkhoz labour force and in reduced need for recruitment of skilled personnel from outside. Furthermore, over and above the state expenditure on education and training, the Kolkhozy themselves have invested substantially in the acquisition and upgrading of skills for their members through sponsoring them in higher level institutions. The Kolkhozy thus have made considerable progress towards achieving self-sufficiency in skills. Many of the earlier shortages of accountants, book-keepers, agronomists and zoo-technicians seem to have been largely overcome. However, because of the vast and continuing expansion of mechanisation, there continue to be shortages of mechanics and other technical personnel.[12] The upsurge in the overall quality of the labour force, particularly of managerial, professional and technical personnel, has resulted in a greatly strengthened capability for planning and absorption of technical advances generated by R and D. The increase in the size of the average Kolkhoz has enabled many of them to employ their own staff of specialists – planners, economists, engineers, accountants, agronomists, mechanics and zoo-technicians. In contrast to the situation in many countries, there does not exist a system of 'agricultural extension services'. Transfer of knowledge from the state-sponsored R and D takes place through other channels such as publications, visits by members of the Kolkhoz to research institutes and experimental demonstration farms and link-up between the Kolkhozy and research institutes.

Finally, there is the question of the role played by the party and the state in determining the organisational structure of the Kolkhoz. The Kolkhoz Charter spells out the organisational framework and rules for the management and operation of its activities. This charter must be adopted by the Kolkhoz members and then approved and registered by the administration. The charters of an individual Kolkhoz are based on the Model Collective Farm Charter of November 1969 which was first approved by the party and the government. The model charter is a comprehensive document and contains provisions on such matters as objectives, membership, rights and obligations of members, utilisation of land and communal property, production and financial planning, labour organisations, remuneration and discipline, distribution of output and income, personal plots and livestock, social security, cultural amenities and public services and administrative bodies. The charters for the individual Kolkhoz are adapted to local conditions but in all essentials, closely follow the model charter.

The preceding discussion on the external framework within which the Kolkhoz must operate can now be summarised. A combination of historical factors and the logic of a centrally planned economy have resulted in a situation where some of the key parameters defining this framework are determined by the state. These include the determination of delivery targets, the procurement price structure, the price and availability of most investment goods and the fixing of minimum wage and certain social welfare services. On the other hand, there has been a trend since 1953 away from direct state control through administrative methods and towards greater autonomy of the Kolkhozy. This trend is represented by such factors as the replacement of detailed specification of physical inputs by contracts incorporating delivery targets and of annual quotas by five year quotas; the development of cost accounting since the mid-1950s; ownership of, and control over, machinery and equipment by the Kolkhozy itself rather than an external agency; greater freedom by the Kolkhozy with respect to the volume and pattern of investment financed either from internal sources or from borrowing; and greater self-sufficiency in managerial, professional and technical skills. It is these changes in the external framework which provide the context for a study of the internal organisation and functioning of the Kolkhozy to which we now turn.

(b) INTERNAL STRUCTURE AND ORGANISATION

Although there are differences of details, the Kolkhozy display remarkable similarity in internal structure and organisation. The main organs of a Kolkhoz are the general meeting, the board, the inspection committee, the brigades and *firmas*. The leadership personnel consist of the chairman and members of the board, the specialist staff and heads of brigades and firmas. The structure of the Kolkhoz may be illustrated by the following organisation chart for Kolkhoz XXII Party Congress in Tajikistan:

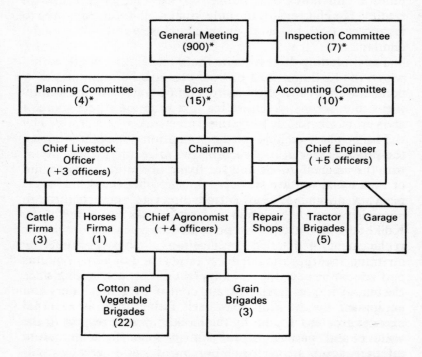

Note: The figures in brackets refer to number of persons (indicated by asterisks where not specifically mentioned as such) or brigades firmas (without asterisks).

The most important body in a Kolkhoz is the *general meeting*. Its membership consists of all the Kolkhozniks. However, in large farms where it may be difficult to hold meetings of the members, the general meeting consists of delegates elected by the members in brigades and other production sub-divisions. Of the five Kolkhozy visited by us, in three – all in Tajikistan – the general meeting consisted of elected delegates, while in the other two, it comprised of all members. This difference is probably the result of the size of the farms. In the former three, the number of households were 2338, 1420 and 1891, while in the latter two, the corresponding figures were 854 and 1045.

The general meeting is convened by the board at least four times a year. Its functions include approval of the charter; election of the chairman and members of the board and inspection commission; membership questions; approval of regulations on payment for work, and of production and financial plans, including distribution and accumulation; approval of the decisions of the board on appointments of senior personnel; and decisions on participation in joint activities with other farms and organisations and on the enlargement or division of the collective farm.[13]

The general meeting elects members of the *auditing or inspection commission* which is charged among other things, with the supervision of the financial and economic transactions of the collective farm. It has a full-time chairman but other members drawn from the general Kolkhoz membership, serve on a part-time basis.

The general meeting also elects members of the *board* which is the executive body of the Kolkhoz and is responsible for directing the organisational, production, financial, cultural and educational activities of the Kolkhoz. Its members are elected for a three-year period and work on a part-time basis except for the chairman who is full-time and is the chief executive of the Kolkhoz. The board membership is quite small, generally varying from 8 to 15 persons. The board meets quite frequently, on average more than once a month. Since in terms of actual policy formulation and implementation the board is the most important Kolkhoz body, its composition is important in determining popular participation in management. In most collective farms, the chief professional officers— agronomist, engineer, economist-accountant—would be members of the board. This pattern was observed in all the Kolkhozy visited by us. Most of them also contained a few ordinary Kolkhozniki as board members. In the Leninism Kolkhoz, out of 15 board members, no less than 11 were ordinary workers. It is not uncommon for the ordinary workers to constitute a majority of the Kolkhoz boards.

The key figure in the Kolkhoz is the board *chairman*. As

chief executive officer, he is responsible, jointly with the board, for formulation and implementation of most of the important policy decisions. He represents the Kolkhoz in all its substantive and formal dealings with the state bodies and other outside organisations. In contrast with earlier practice and the pattern elsewhere, the chairmen of all the Kolkhozy we visited were 'local sons'. Generally, the chairmen are able, knowledgeable and dedicated to their work. Practically all of them had spent years working in the Kolkhoz in various capacities before being elected to their present positions. In Leninism and Kholkabad, the chairman (actually chairwoman for Kholkabad) had worked previously as agronomists. Another characteristic of the chairmen appeared to be the longevity of their service: the chairmen of the Kolkhozy Karl Marx, Rossiya, XXII Party Congress, and Kholkabad, for instance, have been serving for 12, 12, 8 and 7 years respectively. They had all received higher education: the chairman of the Karl Marx Kolkhoz was a graduate of an agricultural college, while his counterparts in Kholkabad and Leninism had trained as agronomists; the chairmen of Rossiya and XXII Party Congress had graduated from the institutes of economics. In general, the material facilities at their disposal were quite impressive. They all had spacious, well-furnished and comfortable offices and reception rooms. They are entitled to a free house and often a free car, and dispose of generous entertainment allowances.

The Kolkhoz board may set up other committees to assist it in its work. In the XXII Party Congress Kolkhoz, whose organisation chart was given earlier, the board has established two additional committees, one concerned with planning and the other with accounts. Both these committees are staffed by specialists—economists, planners, accountants, book-keepers, etc. In general the specialist staff play a key role in the management and operation of Kolkhoz activities; for instance, the chief agronomist, engineer, zoo-technician, etc., work closely with the chairman and the board and are responsible for dealing with all the technical problems falling within their areas of competence. They also supervise the work of production units – brigades for cultivation and machinery and *firmas* for livestock.

Brigades and *firmas* are the main production units. With the expansion in the overall size of the average Kolkhoz over the past three decades, the size of brigades had expanded correspondingly. In many ways, the brigades of today are comparable in size and in respect of some functions with the Kolkhozy of the early 1950s. In general, their importance has increased as a result of the expansion of the size of the Kolkhoz and the increasing complexity of its operations. All the production workers are organised into brigades and *firmas*. They are charged with well-defined tasks—for example, the cultivation of so many acres of grain, cotton or vegetables, the raising of livestock, or the operation and maintenance of tractors. Some brigades – the so-called 'complex brigades'— may combine several of these tasks.

The duties of these production units include organisation of work, assignment of daily tasks, quality control, supervision of equipment, fulfilment of production targets, keeping records of work done and the payment of workers. They may make proposals concerning technological change, productivity improvements or payment schemes. However, they do not have powers to set production targets or evolve their own payment and incentive schemes. Each brigade is led by an elected or appointed brigadier. This is generally a full-time job and entails responsibility for the fulfilment of tasks outlined above. Typically each brigade will have an elected council of six to eight members. The brigade is not just a unit for carrying out physical production tasks. It is also a forum for discussion of all matters pertaining to the Kolkhoz. The brigadiers are expected to discuss in advance all matters coming up before the general meeting and to report the decisions of the general meeting and the board to brigade members.

The brigades vary a good deal in size. In the Rossiya Kolkhoz, for example, field brigades comprise 30 to 60 members, and firmas 30 to 35, while tractor brigades have 50 members. Of the five Kolkhozy we visited, the average number of workers per brigade varies from a low of 53 in Rossiya to a high of 103 in Karl Marx.[14]

Zvenos are sub-units of brigades and *firmas*. These are generally rather small—comprising two to six members—and are assigned rather specific tasks. Their members usually work on seasonal or temporary assignments and the unit ceases to function once a given task has been performed. While there has been a great deal of discussion in the Soviet Union and in the other literature on the Kolkhozy about the merits and demerits of zvenos, and while they clearly operate in some regions of the country, they are quite rare in Tajikistan and Uzbekistan. Of the farms visited by us, it was only in Kholkabad that they played some limited and periodic role in production. They were engaged in such tasks as growing of fodder or watering plants and consisted of two or three persons.

To complete the picture, mention should be made of *inter-Kolkhoz* and other joint enterprises. They have grown rapidly in recent years and are strongly supported by the highest leadership and policy-making organs in the country.[15] They represent relatively new forms of organisation involving co-operation in production and services among the Kolkhozy and between the Kolkhozy and state farms or other types of state enterprises. Just as brigades and, sometimes, zvenos seek to enhance efficiency by dividing up the work into smaller production units, the inter-Kolkhoz enterprises represent an attempt at further specialisation and exploitation of economies of scale. They are also a means of utilisation of idle labour time during off-season periods in agricultural cycle and represent another step in 'the complete industrialisation of agriculture'. Lastly, they are a possible forerunner of a new, more advanced form of social property. Under this type of organisation, two or more Kolkhozy come together to operate a new activity, jointly appoint the management board and share profits in accordance with the contributions made.

Their importance and growth in recent years at the national level is brought out in Table 3.4. It will be seen that they are especially prominent in building and construction, followed by animal breeding, poultry farming, forestry and silage. Other activities which lend themselves to such co-operative enterprises include artificial insemination, manufacture of building materials, machinery repairs and processing of farm products.

Such joint enterprises existed in all the Kolkhozy we visited. For instance, Kolkhoz Karl Marx participated in inter-Kolkhoz enterprises concerned with building and livestock,

TABLE 3.4: Number of Interfarm Enterprises and Organisations Belonging
to State and Collective Farms in 1970 and 1975

	1970	1975
Total interfarm enterprises, organisations and associations	4,554	6,327
Areas of Activity:		
building	2,432	2,739
building materials	146	141
forestry	288	465
silage	77	415
processing of farm products	14	29
animal breeding	272	591
poultry farming	574	556
artificial insemination	57	194
diversified enterprises	299	241
Others	395	956

Source: T. Khachaturov, *The Economy of the Soviet Union Today* p. 266 (Moscow: Progress Publishers, 1977).

Kolkhoz Leninism engaged in joint projects for cattle breeding and machine repairs and Kolkhoz Kholkabad for making apple juice.

(c) PARTICIPATION AND DECISION-MAKING

It is an inherently difficult task to assess participation and the process of decision-making in an organisation. It is difficult to devise statistics and other 'objective' data to measure intangibles such as participation and decision-making. And indirect indicators in this area are difficult to come by. The difficulties are further compounded by the fact that in any organisation, there is generally a gap—sometimes a very considerable one—between the reality and the rules. Thus any proper analysis of participation and decision-making must be based on a prolonged and intensive study of the organisation and must employ various kinds of research methodology, including participant-observation. Our study was not designed to explore issues of participation and decision-making. Given the complexity of doing work in this area and the constraints of time, language and other factors within which we were operating, it would have been exceedingly unwise to have launched an enquiry of this nature. Nevertheless, the themes of participation and decision-making are of intense contemporary interest and it may, therefore, be useful to put down our tentative observations in this area.

The first point to make on participation is that the sheer size of the modern Kolkhozy rules out direct and continuous participation by peasants in the running of the farm. The average number of households in a Kolkhoz on an all-Union basis is slightly less than 500. In the farms visited by us, the numbers ranged from 854 in Kolkhoz Leninism to 2338 in Kolkhoz Karl Marx. Participation, therefore, has to be through other means such as elections to planning and decision-making organs and decentralisation of powers to lower echelon bodies where direct participation is feasible.

As mentioned earlier, in a Kolkhoz the key body which is ultimately responsible for decisions on all major policy issues is the general meeting which consists either of all the Kolkhozniki or of delegates elected by them. The general meeting must be convened at least four times a year. While this provides an opportunity to the rank and file members to participate directly in decision-making, given the complex and technical nature of many of the issues involved and the size of the meeting, it is doubtful whether the general meeting can be an effective vehicle for popular participation. This is, of course, not to deny that critical opinions are often expressed at these meetings on policy decisions taken by the board or, in extreme cases, the members exercise their rights to dismiss the chairman or members of the board. In terms of the control of the activities of the Kolkhozy, the inspection commission, which is selected by the general meeting and is independent of the Kolkhoz board, can be more effective.

The principal methods available for popular participation in the management of the Kolkoz are through elections of delegates to various policy-making bodies and discussions in brigades. As for the first method, it was noted above that the chairman and members of the board, members of the brigade councils (where they exist) and brigadiers (sometimes) are elective posts. The key policy-making body in the Kolkhoz is the board. It is the board which takes day-to-day decisions on all major policy issues and reports to the general meeting. Its effective power is further strengthened by its access to specialist knowledge and skills either directly through board members or by its ability to call upon the other professional and technical staff.

Another avenue for participation in decision-making is provided by meetings of the brigades and the firmas. It appears that meetings at this level are held frequently. Although some brigades are already of a size to make effective participation difficult, others with a membership around 40 or 50 provide suitable institutional framework. These meetings provide an occasion for discussion of matters both of the type which falls within the purview of the brigades and the firmas as well as of those coming up for consideration in the board and the general meeting. Given the importance of brigade-level meetings for the exercise of Kolkhoz democracy, the decentralisation of decision-making down to this level becomes an instrument for enhancing popular participation. In this respect, as noted earlier, the brigades dispose of relatively little power for decision-making on important policy matters. This may be illustrated by a discussion of the decision-making power in three key areas: decisions on what, how much and how to produce; on payment systems and determination of rates, differentials and bonuses; and finally, on division between distribution and accumulation and on investment patterns. In the determination of policy in all these matters, the state and the party play a considerable role. They do this in a variety of ways; for instance, by influencing Kolkhoz production decisions, by fixing quotas and procurement prices, or by issuing guidelines and norms affecting decisions on payment methods, remuneration structures, and amount and pattern of investment. In the areas of policy open to the Kolkhoz, the decisions on the above matters are made effectively by the board though the general meeting must ultimately endorse these decisions for them to be valid.

4 Production and Accumulation in Collective Agriculture

1. INTRODUCTION

In this chapter an attempt will be made to evaluate the economic performance of the Kolkhoz system in the Soviet Central Asia. We shall mainly look at the productive efficiency of the collective farms and comment briefly on the internal rate of accumulation.

As in the earlier chapters, we set out to derive results that would generally apply to the whole of the Central Asian economic region but our data frequently refer to Uzbekistan and Tajikistan. Besides the measurements for these two republics we would often refer to the data for the five collective farms—three in Tajikistan and two in Uzbekistan—that we visited. It will be clear that in many ways these collective farms differed significantly from the average. But we were able to generate some detailed information with respect to their operation. Such information, duly qualified, should be useful in helping understand the working of the collective agriculture in the region.

2. PRODUCTIVE EFFICIENCY

(a) THE SUCCESS STORY OF COTTON

Critics frequently indict Soviet agricultural performance for low factor productivity. As we have already discussed, this critique does not apply to cotton, the overwhelmingly dominant product of Central Asian agriculture, so long as output per hectare is used as the indicator.[1] By all standards the achievement in terms of output per hectare has been remarkable. In comparison with the pre-revolutionary level of 1.22 tons (and only about 0.8 ton in the beginning of the 1930s) the output of raw cotton per hectare reached the level of three tons in 1976. Table 4.1 shows that the Central Asian republics have the highest rate of yield per hectare of all the significant producers of cotton in the world. Even within the USSR these republics, which supply the bulk of the cotton, are far above the rest in terms of yield per unit of land.

TABLE 4.1: Major Cotton Producers of the World, 1976

Country	Total Production (Thousand Tons of Lint Equivalent)	Yield per hectare (Tons of Raw Cotton)
USSR	2800	2.82
China	2400	1.47
USA	2298	1.35
(Uzbekistan)	(1800)	(3.00)
India	1146	0.46
Pakistan	515	0.84
Turkey	470	2.10
Brazil	390	0.66
Egypt	386	1.95
(Tajikistan)	(288)	(3.00)
(Turkmenistan)	(356)	(2.13)
(Kirghizia)	(71)	(2.88)
Total World	12695	1.16

Note: Uzbek, Tajik and USSR data have been quoted from *NK SU 60*. Data for the other countries have been compiled from FAO, *Production Yearbook*, Vol. 30, Rome 1977.

For the world as a whole the ratio of lint to raw cotton is about 0.35. For the USSR the ratio is 0.34. These ratios have been used to convert raw cotton into lint (and *vice versa*) in deriving the figures shown in the table. In 1976 only three countries showed higher than the USSR rate of yield per hectare. These were: Guatemala (3.35 tons), Israel (3.21 tons) and Sri Lanka (3.00 tons). Each of them is a small producer. Their outputs, in lint equivalent, were respectively 100,000, 50,000 and 2,000 tons.

In the five collective farms that the authors visited the yield per hectare was, on the average, higher than that for the republics. But these farms, on the average, were not far out of line with the average for the republics.[2]

(b) RELATIVE PERFORMANCE OF KOLKHOZ AND SOVKHOZ IN GROWING COTTON

Table 4.2 provides some information about the relative performance of Kolkhoz and Sovkhoz within these republics in the production of cotton. The performance of the collective farms is respectively 29 and 26 per cent better in Uzbekistan and Tajikistan in terms of output per unit of land as compared with that in the state farms. In terms of the officially reported unit cost of production, a concept whose contents are not clearly defined, the collective farms have 5 per cent advantage in Uzbekistan and 4 per cent disadvantage in Tajikistan in comparison with the state farms. Direct labour cost is higher in the collective farms, as compared with the state farms, by a quarter or more.

TABLE 4.2: Yield and Cost of Cotton in Kolkhoz and Sovkhoz in Uzbekistan and Tajikistan

	Uzbekistan		Tajikistan	
	Kolkhoz	Sovkhoz	Kolkhoz	Sovkhoz
Output per hectare (tons of raw cotton)	3.30	2.56	3.08	2.45
Cost of production (rubles per ton)	417	441	467	450
Direct Labour cost (Man hours per ton)	330	260	400	320

Note: Figures showing yield per hectare in Tajikistan are for 1973. All the other figures are for 1976. Sovkhoz figures include a small amount produced by 'other state enterprises'. Cost of production and direct labour cost are quoted from *NK SU 60*. The definition of these concepts, beyond what is implied by the terminology employed, is not spelled out in any detail. Outputs per hectare have been estimated from the data shown in *NK Uz. 60* and *ST 50*.

Table 4.3 shows some interesting facts about the relative levels of mechanisation of the collective and state farms. In terms of tractorisation (i.e., tractors per unit of land) the

TABLE 4.3: Mechanisation of Kolkhoz and Sovkhoz in Uzbekistan and Tajikistan

	Uzbekistan (1976)		Tajikistan (1973)	
	Kolkhoz	Sovkhoz	Kolkhoz	Sovkhoz
No. of Tractors per thousand hectares of sown land	47	30	34	30
Cotton Harvesters per thousand hectares of cotton land	15	20	10	13
No. of workers per tractor	13	10	16	11

Source: The estimates have been based on the data shown in *NK Uz. 60* and *ST 50*.

collective farms are significantly more mechanised than the state farms in the two republics. In both the republics the level of tractorisation is way above that for the USSR as a whole where an average collective farm had 11 tractors per thousand hectares of sown land in 1976. Since agriculture as a whole in the USSR also had the same level of tractorisation it would appear that at the all-Union level the rate of tractorisation of the Sovkhozy was about the same.[3] What is even more surprising is that the overall rate of tractorisation in Central Asian agriculture would appear to have been greater than that in the highly capital-intensive agriculture in the USA. In 1972 in the USA there were 33 tractors per thousand hectares of cropland.[4] Whether this comparison means an effectively higher rate of tractorisation of agriculture (especially of the collective farms) or merely a less efficient rate of use of these machines in Central Asia as compared with the USA is something that can be determined only after a good deal of additional information becomes available.

Although the Sovkhozy, as compared to the Kolkhozy, have fewer tractors per unit of land they have more tractors per worker. Also, in terms of tractors per worker, an average Kolkhoz in the USSR, with a score of 14 farm workers per tractor, is no less capital-intensive than their Central Asian counterparts. Agriculture as a whole in the USSR, with 10 workers per tractor, is somewhat more capital-intensive than that in Central Asia according to this criterion. In comparison in the USA in 1972 there was one tractor per worker.[5]

The crucial advantage that the Sovkhozy have over the Kolkhozy in terms of the mechanisation of cotton growing is their access to about a third more of harvesters per hectare. In terms of harvesters *per worker* the Sovkhozy have even greater advantage over the Kolkhozy. This must be the major explanation for the much lower direct labour cost of producing cotton in the Sovkhozy. Manual cotton picking is still widespread at the Kolkhozy and this is a highly labour-intensive process.[6]

One may want to summarise the relative performance of the Kolkhozy and the Sovkhozy in growing cotton in Central Asia by highlighting the following points:

(i) Output per unit of land is unambiguously higher at the Kolkhozy by more than a quarter on the average.

(ii) Output per unit of labour is about 25 per cent higher at the Sovkhoz.

(iii) The evidence about cost of production is less unambiguous, but the weighted average of such cost would appear to be somewhat lower for the Kolkhozy.

(iv) The greater labour-productivity at the Sovkhozy is probably explained largely by their greater capital-intensity (measured as the amount of capital equipment per worker) and the more balanced composition of capital equipment (as reflected in the relative availability of tractors and harvesters).

(v) The higher output per unit of land at the Kolkhozy has been achieved at the cost of employing a good deal more of labour to each hectare.

One may tentatively conclude that the lower output per worker at the Kolkhozy is a reflection of the diminishing returns arising out of the more intensive application of labour and a somewhat unbalanced composition of capital equipment (in the form of too few harvesters and, perhaps, too many tractors).

What can one say about the relative efficiency of the two forms of organisation in growing cotton? Not much in the absence of a good deal more of information. If prices were accurate reflections of social scarcity and if costs were comprehensively accounted for, then one could argue that the lower cost of production at the Kolkhozy is a testimony to their greater efficiency.[7] It is, unfortunately, difficult to argue that either of these conditions has been fulfilled.[8]

Again, if one knew that land were relatively scarce and labour relatively abundant, then the performance of the Kolkhozy would appear to be superior. There are powerful considerations to suggest that such may indeed be the case. In spite of its vast geographical expanse Central Asia is in short supply of cultivable land. In 1976, in Uzbekistan, there were only 1.6 hectares of cultivated land per Kolkhoz worker. This was less than a quarter of the corresponding figure for the USSR. Indeed, the amount is lower than the available amount of land per agricultural worker in Pakistan. In Tajikistan the amount of cultivated land per Kolkhoz worker is 1.9 hectares—only a little higher than in Uzbekistan. Although actual figures are not available, it appears that an augmentation in the supply of cultivated land is very costly in terms of resources. Expensive irrigation projects have to be undertaken to bring new land under cultivation.

On the other hand, one could argue on the basis of the discussion in Chapter 2 that the supply of labour is probably now less of a constraint. The rate of population growth has been accelerating in the recent past and, as yet, there is no sign of deceleration in growth. The region has a positive rate of net immigration. Thus, in years to come, the rate of increase in labour supply is likely to accelerate for some time at least.

If the above characterisation of the relative factor supply is an approximately correct description of the situation in Central Asia, then one would justifiably attribute greater efficiency to the Kolkhozy than to the Sovkhozy. It is, however, uncertain how accurate the above characterisation is. A possible alternative hypothesis is that the existing allocation of labour is not dictated by the conditions of supply in relation to production possibilities but by the circumstances dictated by the lack of adequate supply of farm equipment.

Agriculture in Central Asia is generally more labour-intensive than agriculture in the USSR as a whole. Compared to the leading agriculture in the world in terms of labour-productivity, that of the United States, labour input in Central Asian agriculture is staggeringly high. But the evidence compiled in Table 4.4 shows that the Central Asian collective farms have a *relatively* higher labour productivity in cotton than in grain or livestock when their performance is compared with the Soviet or US agriculture. Thus, compared with the average in the US during the mid-1960s Uzbek collective farms a decade later needed 19 times labour per unit of grain and 10 times per unit of cattle but only 6 times per unit of cotton. The ratios are broadly similar for Tajikistan.

It is only natural that Central Asian agriculture, having an endowment of relative resources very different from the average for the USSR and the USA, would use much more of labour per unit of land and thereby have a lower output per unit of labour. But, to ensure continued progress in the living standard of the rural population, it will be necessary to improve output per worker by reducing labour requirement per unit of cotton and for other agricultural produce.

As we discussed in an earlier chapter the extraordinarily favourable treatment that cotton received from domestic price policy in the past has gradually been eroded. It is unlikely that cotton will ever be restored to the kind of relative advantage it enjoyed in the past. Thus, output per worker must increase if cotton growers are to continue to obtain increases in real income. One of the measures that would be necessary to promote this goal is a more balanced mechanisation of cotton growing at the Kolkhoz. It would be necessary to invest in equipment for harvesting and, perhaps, reduce the need to carry the heavy inventory of tractors by improving the efficiency of using the latter.

(c) RELATIVE INCENTIVE FOR COTTON AND GRAIN

This is perhaps the place to go into the question that we asked in Chapter 2: did the policy-induced specialisation in cotton in Central Asia go beyond the dictates of economic efficiency? It is not possible to arrive at any definitive conclusion in the absence of detailed knowledge of relative scarcities of specific resources and products from the standpoint of the society. But

TABLE 4.4: Labour Requirement Per Ton of Cotton, Grain and Cattle
(man hours)

	Kolkhoz: USSR	Kolkhoz: Uzbekistan	Kolkhoz: Tajikistan	USA (1963–7)	Uzbek ÷ USA	Tajik ÷ USA
Grain	14	74	88	4	18.5	22.0
Raw Cotton	350	330	400	56	5.9	7.1
Cattle	560	690	690	70	9.9	9.9

Note: Data for USSR and its republics are for 1976 and quoted from *NK SU 60*. The US data are the averages for 1963–7 and quoted from US Department of Agriculture, *Agricultural Statistics*, 1968, Washington, DC, 1968.

one can try to hypothesise on the basis of the partial information available.

In Chapter 2 it was shown that even as recently as in 1976 the average procurement price for cotton was probably a higher proportion of international cotton price than the average procurement price of grain was in relation to international grain price.[9] On this basis one might be tempted to argue that the profitability of cotton was being artificially kept high relative to that of grain, the main competing crop. Had this not been the case there would have been a reduction in cotton growing and an increase in grain production.

Such a conclusion would appear to be unwarranted once the full complexity of the Soviet system of procurement is taken into account. The procurement price of a product is not uniform all over the USSR, or even within each republic. For grain, for example, there are 17 procurement zones in the USSR. The lowest price is offered to the Krasnodar zone where the natural conditions are best and cost of production lowest. The highest price is paid to the producers in the far eastern zone where natural conditions are worst and cost highest. For cotton there are three procurement zones within the Uzbek Republic alone. Price is lowest for Ferghana-Tashkent zone where conditions are best and highest in the semi-arid Karakalpak-Bokhara zone where conditions are worst.[10]

As is well-known there is no land rent in the USSR. From what is known about the principle of differentiating procurement prices between regions it appears that this practice is a substitute for land rent in preventing polarisation in regional income inequality arising out of vast regional differences in the quality of land. Had procurement prices been uniform, the differential rent of land in a fertile region would have augmented the income of the workers of the region. This is a benefit from which the workers in a less fertile region would be excluded. Differential procurement pricing is a mechanism to siphon off such differential rent. In principle, it could serve as a generalised tool of regional income equalisation to offset the extremes of inequality arising out of differences in resource endowment. It should, however, be noted that translating into practice what is possible in principle is by no means an easy task. To set procurement prices for many products in many regions and yet not distort relative incentives away from the socially desirable pattern must be very difficult.

Table 4.5 shows the average procurement prices for cotton and grain in the republic of Uzbekistan in recent years.

TABLE 4.5: Change in Price/Cost Ratio for Cotton and Grain in Uzbekistan

	1965	1970	1975	1976
Average procurement price (rubles/ton)				
Cotton	435.6	539.8	544.0	561.6
Grain	159.7	157.0	172.2	150.6
Index of procurement price with international price = 100				
Cotton	–	–	–	127
Grain	–	–	–	150
Ratio of the unit price of cotton to the unit price of grain				
Uzbekistan	–	–	–	3.73
International	–	–	–	4.63
Average cost of production in Kolkhoz (rubles/ton)				
Cotton	310	384	413	417
Grain	140	122.7	180.0	117.7
Price to cost ratio				
Cotton	1.41	1.41	1.32	1.35
Grain	1.14	1.28	0.96	1.28
Kolkhoz profit per ton (rubles)				
Cotton	–	–	–	144.6
Grain	–	–	–	32.9
Kolkhoz profit per hectare (rubles)				
Cotton	–	–	–	433.8
Grain	–	–	–	55.6
Kolkhoz profit per man-hour (rubles)				
Cotton	–	–	–	1.31
Grain	–	–	–	0.75

Following the general principle described above, the price of cotton has been set a little lower than all-Union average (to reflect the favourable conditions for cotton production in Uzbekistan) and the price of grain has been set way above the all Union level (to allow for the unfavourable conditions of grain production).[11] A fairly crude comparison reveals that by 1976 these procurement prices meant a higher degree of 'protection' for grain than for cotton in the republic – a result which is the exact opposite of the result for the Union as a whole. The average procurement price of cotton was 27 per cent above the international price while that of grain was 50 per cent above.[12] It would, therefore, appear that relative incentives within the republic are not turned against the dictates of economic efficiency in favour of cotton. Even so, cotton, on the average, remains the crop with higher return per hectare and per worker.

The above analysis would appear to have left a number of questions unresolved. For example, why does cotton not encroach further into grain land if the above figures are reasonable approximations of reality? A number of factors could account for this. First, in analysing such a phenomenon one should look at the marginal, rather than average, conditions. At the margin land is probably quite unsuitable to cotton since, over the decades, grain was gradually pushed out of better land. Secondly, the figures in Table 4.5 are the averages for the republic which has a number of zones for each crop. The differential levels of prices in these zones could easily have produced an 'equilibrium' with the average conditions as represented by the figures in Table 4.5. Finally, the determining ratio may be more complex than the simple calculation of profit per hectare or per worker.

As already mentioned, part of the reason the productivity of grain is low and its cost high is that the past historical bias in favour of cotton gradually pushed grain out of better land. Now the levels of relative prices have been substantially reversed to make grain production in such unfavourable conditions reasonably profitable. Why then, one may ask, do the collectives not find it more profitable to reverse some of the historical process and go back to the cultivation of grain on better land? In the absence of more detailed information all one can do is to cite the same factors that have been mentioned in the above paragraph. It is also likely that administrative influence and campaign play major roles in obviating too sharp a response to incentives, especially when these incentives, resulting from too complicated and intractable a system of controls, tend to contradict more directly expressed goals.

One final aspect of the cotton economy is sufficiently interesting to deserve some discussion. The Soviet Union has long been a major exporter of cotton. In recent years it has been the second largest exporter of cotton closely following the USA. Indeed, in the 1975–76 trade year it exceeded the USA in gross aggregate exports. In 1976 gross Soviet exports amounted to 32 per cent of domestic production and 23 per cent of world exports.[13] It is not known at what unit price Soviet cotton is exported abroad, but it seems reasonable to assume that such price would be the same as the one ruling in the world market.[14] Average procurement price has, however, been about 32 per cent above international price. If the costs of storage and marketing are added, then it would appear that the Soviet authorities may have been paying out 50 to 60 per cent more than their receipts from exports. While we have all along recognised the possibility of significant error in these calculations we cannot imagine that all or the main part of this estimate can be attributed to such error.

It is probable that the planners value foreign exchange highly enough to make such a policy acceptable. If, however, the appropriate exchange rate of the ruble is anything like what is implied by it, then, at the all-Union average level (though not at the Central Asian republics), grain would appear to have been deprived of a high enough procurement price that would be warranted by such an exchange rate even in as recent a year as 1976.

(d) GRAIN CROPS

Up to this point the discussion of productive efficiency has been centred around cotton. This is natural in view of the overwhelming importance of this crop in Central Asia. It is, however, of some interest to have a quick look at the performance in grain crops. These are, admittedly, grown in many areas on relatively inferior land.

Table 4.6 shows their yield per hectare. In each republic of Central Asia there has been very large increase in output of grain per hectare over the recent decades. The rate of increase has been phenomenal in recent years. A good deal of it must have been the result of the policy of improving incentives for grain cultivation. During the 1960s the yield rate in these republics, with the exception of Kirghizia, ranged between 60 and 70 per cent of that in the USSR as a whole. By 1976 the average yield rate in Central Asia was above that for the USSR, and Tajikistan—a minor producer contributing less than 8 per cent of the region's grain output—was the only Central Asian republic that lagged significantly behind the all-Union average. This was a remarkable act of catching up.

TABLE 4.6: Grain Yield Per Hectare in Metric Tons

	1940	Average 1961–5	Average 1966–70	Average 1971–5	1976
USSR	0.86	1.02	1.37	1.47	1.75
Central Asia					
Average	–	–	–	–	1.82
Uzbekistan	0.41	0.67	0.74	0.95	1.69
Tajikistan	0.57	0.61	0.66	0.83	1.14
Kirghizia	0.76	1.02	1.56	1.87	2.28
Turkmenistan	0.57	0.72	0.86	1.40	2.10
All Asia	–	–	–	–	1.69
India	–	–	–	–	1.22
Iran	–	–	–	–	1.27
Iraq	–	–	–	–	0.97
Pakistan	–	–	–	–	1.44
Turkey	–	–	–	–	1.89
Afghanistan	–	–	–	–	1.31

Source: Soviet data quoted from: *NK SU 60*. The rest quoted from FAO, *Production Yearbook*, Vol. 30, 1977.

Productivity per hectare in Central Asia is still way below the rates achieved by Japan (5.28 tons per hectare), Korea (3 in North and 4.5 in South), Europe (3.1) and North-Central America (3.1). But compared with its more immediate Asian neighbours the performance of these republics must be rated as highly satisfactory.

We do not have separate data about productivity of grain per hectare in the Kolkhozy and the Sovkhozy. Table 4.7 shows unit costs of production and direct labour inputs into grain in these two forms of organisation. The general pattern is the same as in the case of cotton: cost of production is significantly lower (Turkmenistan is the only exception), while direct labour input is higher (Tajikistan and Kirghizia are the exceptions, but each by a relatively small margin) at the Kolkhozy. It would appear that the lower cost of production at the Kolkhozy, despite a much higher (but in the case of Tajikistan and Kirghizia marginally lower) labour input, is probably the result of higher output per hectare. One would tend to conclude that all that has been said about the relative efficiency of the Kolkhozy and the Sovkhozy in connection with cotton would substantially apply to their relative perform-ance in grain production although, in the absence of direct measurements of output per hectare in the two systems, one would feel even less certain.

TABLE 4.7: Relative Performance of Kolkhoz and Sovkhoz in Grain Production

	Cost of Production (rubles per ton)		Direct Labour Input (man-hours per ton)	
	Kolkhoz	*Sovkhoz*	*Kolkhoz*	*Sovkhoz*
Uzbekistan	118	149	74	43
Tajikistan	129	139	88	91
Kirghizia	62	72	21	25
Turkmenistan	120	103	58	27

Source: *NK SU 60*. The figures are for 1976.

3. COLLECTIVE AGRICULTURE AND PERSONAL PLOTS

The issue of personal plots has been a controversial one in the context of Soviet agricultural development. The performance of this sector has been the basis of criticism levelled against the Soviet system both from the right and the left. Western economists have long argued that the personal plots have a much higher output per hectare than collective agriculture. This, according to such economists, is an undisputed testimony to the greater efficiency of private, as compared with collective, agriculture. The critique from the left has been based on the argument that the continuation and prosperity of personal plots is inconsistent with the avowed objective of transition to communism – a society in which distribution should be based on need and not on the unequal entitlements based on unequal capacities to produce.

The Soviet answer to these critics has been to claim that the produce of personal plots, as a proportion of total marketed farm output, has been declining and that by now this sector is not of much quantitative significance. Unfortunately, the scanty time series data published by the official sources refer to the USSR as a whole.[15] Our discussion about Central Asia must be based on the small amount of data that we have amassed for the five Kolkhozy and comparative figures of aggregative nature for the republics. These data are shown in Table 6.1 in Chapter 6.

Personal plots in the Central Asian Kolkhoz are on the average much smaller than the ones in the rest of the USSR. The average size in Uzbekistan and Tajikistan are respectively 0.12 and 0.13 hectare as compared to 0.33 in the USSR. This is probably due to the relatively adverse land to man ratio in Central Asian agriculture – a fact to which reference has already been made. The average size of a personal plot in the five Kolkhoz is 0.14 hectares which is marginally higher than the corresponding averages for the two republics.

If the data about the five Kolkhozy are anything to go by, the contribution of personal plots to family income is by no means small. Income from a personal plot, including self-consumption, varies rather widely – from 18 to 40 per cent of the total household income defined to include income from the following sources: collective Kolkhoz labour, outside employment and personal plot. However, items such as imputed rental value of owner-occupied house and collective consumption are excluded from this definition of total household income. There is perfect negative rank correlation between this ratio and family income from collective Kolkhoz labour.

Although the 'sample' is very small one is tempted to note a strong negative association between high collective prosperity and low income from personal plots.

Value of output per hectare in a private plot is, on the average, more than four times as much as the value of output on collectively farmed land. There is a lot of variation even for our very small 'sample', however. This is a ratio that needs to be explained and understood clearly.

The produce of collective farms is largely sold to the state at fixed prices. The state in turn sells these goods at controlled prices to the urban and rural buyers through state retail outlets. The produce of private plots does not have to follow the same route. They can be taken by the Kolkhozniki to the 'Kolkhoz markets' in nearby towns. At these markets prices are freely determined by the interaction between buyers and sellers. It is well known that prices at these Kolkhoz markets are higher than the prices ruling at the state shops, often located on the same premises, frequently by as much as two to three times. Thus, even if output per hectare were the same on collective and personal land, the *value* of output, defined in this case as the actual sale proceeds, would be greater for the personal plots.

How could one explain the difference in prices? One possibility is shortage and consequent rationing at the state retail shops. This is probably responsible for a good part of the price difference between the state shops and Kolkhoz markets. The difference in revenue due to this factor must be seen as the result of concealed tax on collective production by the state procurement machinery – a tax that is passed to the consumers as a subsidy through the state retail shops.

But a good part of the difference in price is due to the inherent difficulty on the part of a centralised procurement and marketing agency in dealing with certain goods of perishable nature. Thus, one is struck by the remarkable quality difference between the state shops and Kolkhoz markets for vegetables, fruits and similar items. Price difference is highest for these products.[16] Sometimes the high revenue is due to the non-competitive nature of the goods, for example home-processed food, sold by the Kolkhozniki.[17]

To the extent the difference in revenue is due to such factors one must treat the higher revenue from personal plots as return to the Kolkhozniki labour as traders and manufacturers. Indeed, there seems to be a tendency on the part of the personal plots to specialise in the goods in which such activities add a good deal to retail prices. Thus, in the case of the five collective farms there seemed to exist a pattern of specialisation in items like vegetables and fruits.

It must be recognised that even if the factors noted above were absent, there would be a tendency for the Kolkhozniki to apply greater effort to personal plots if they wanted to have a higher overall return for their labour. This is because the value added by collective labour is subject to deductions in the form of tax, collective accumulation and provision for social services. The weighted average of the ratios of labour payment to value added in the five collective farms was 0.69. Thus, even if an individual Kolkhoznik has no additional uncertainty about the process of collective production, he would allocate his effort between collective and personal plots in a way that the product of the marginal unit is lower in the latter. As a result labour input and volume of output would tend to be greater per unit of personal plot than per unit of collective land.[18]

4. ACCUMULATION

We have discussed how Central Asian agriculture had in the past been subjected to a very low rate of surplus extraction as compared to that in the rest of the USSR. Direct taxation of Kolkhoz income in Central Asia continues to be low. The weighted average rate of income tax in the five Kolkhozy was 4.1 per cent of value added in 1976. The highest rate of 6.6 per cent obtained in the prosperous Kolkhoz Kholkabad while Kolkhoz XXII Party Congress, because of its low rate of profit, paid no taxes at all.

Whether the terms of trade between collective agriculture and the state is a mechanism that represents a concealed tax or not is very difficult to say. To establish criteria for quantifying such extraction of surplus is extremely difficult. Even if one could agree about such principles, the inadequacy of available information would make it impossible to apply them. The burden of our preceding discussion, however, has been to show that the prices received by the products of collective agriculture in Central Asia probably represent no substantial degree of concealed taxation. Whether such taxation is substantially incorporated in the prices of the products sold to agriculture or not is less certain.

Whatever the amount the state extracts on the aggregate must be balanced against substantial state contribution to the collective consumption and investment of the Kolkhoz. Contribution to collective consumption takes the form of payments for teachers, doctors and staff at the Kolkhoz schools and hospitals and major share of the costs of pensions and family support allowances. Contribution to investment consists of the financing of large-scale irrigation and land improvement projects.

To the extent the authors were able to determine, it is not the usual practice to charge the users for the water or other benefits of such state-financed projects. Yet another form of state contribution is cheap, long-term credit to finance capital investment. The rate of interest on such credit is only 1 per cent, while the repayment period can be as long as 20 years.

On the whole the collective agriculture in Central Asia would appear to be making a fairly low, if any, aggregate transfer to the state. The inadequacy of information on which the conclusion is based has been repeatedly emphasised by the present writers. But the burden of available evidence does not lead one to conclude with any certainty that the situation is anything like a substantial rate of 'primitive socialist accumulation' imposed on agriculture.

The information that we have about the savings and investment behaviour of collective agriculture refers only to the five Kolkhozy. The weighted averages of the relevant magnitudes for the five Kolkhozy were as follows for 1976 (all percentages of value added):

Total investment	21.1
Increase in reserve	3.1
Internal saving by Kolkhoz	20.4
Gross long-term borrowing from credit institutions	3.8

The rate of investment is quite high especially when one considers the fact that this excludes any large-scale development project that the state might have undertaken. Internal saving rate is also very high—over 20 per cent of value added. While three of the five Kolkhozy borrowed from the financial institutions the weighted average of *net* borrowing for all the five Kolkhozy was less than one per cent of value added.

Behind the average picture depicted above there was considerable variation among the five collective farms. Saving rate ranged from 10 per cent to 30 per cent of value added and the rate of investment from 14 per cent to 41 per cent (see Table 4.1). Over a single year such variation is to be expected for enterprises engaged in an inherently volatile activity as agriculture. What would be useful to know is whether the weighted average for the five Kolkhozy is a reasonable approximation of the behaviour of the collective agriculture in Central Asia. This, unfortunately, we do not know.

5 Income Distribution and Social Consumption

1. INTRODUCTION

In Chapter 2 the growth in per capita national and sectoral incomes in Uzbekistan and Tajikistan were analysed and compared with the corresponding trends for the USSR as a whole. The analysis was conducted in aggregative terms. In this chapter an attempt will be made to discuss some aspects of the distribution of income and social consumption at the Kolkhoz level. The discussion will be based for the most part on the information collected by the authors in the course of their field visit. Unfortunately, there is no comprehensive data published on the distribution of income among the Kolkhozy or rural households in Soviet Central Asia. It is, therefore, not possible to arrive at any overall measure of income distribution (for example, the shares of decile or quintile groups, Gini coefficients, etc.) for all rural households and to make comparisons with the performance of other systems.

The official criterion of income payments in a Kolkhoz, as in the Soviet society, is to make them proportional to quantity and quality of work performed. This is justified by the need to provide material incentives. But the inherent and acquired differences in the ability to work, reinforced by different levels of need arising out of differences in family size, dependency ratio and such other factors, may easily lead to substantial differences in per capita income between households. The main role of social consumption is to counter the extreme effects of this phenomenon by ensuring a minimum level of consumption with respect to such services as health, education, housing and culture. Although the necessary quantitative data do not exist to provide the required evidence, it seems beyond any reasonable doubt that the items of social consumption are fairly equitably distributed. Within a Kolkhoz their distribution is highly equal and between different Kolkhozy these services, an overwhelming proportion of which is financed by contributions from the state, are almost certainly less unequal than production or per capita income. Thus the effect of social consumption is to diminish personal, family and regional inequalities in income and consumption.

2. THE DISTRIBUTION OF INCOME

(a) THE DEGREE OF INEQUALITY BETWEEN COLLECTIVE FARMS

Even with the limited variation in the natural conditions of the five collective farms that the authors visited a good deal of inequality in average incomes and earnings can be observed. The basic information has been summarised in Table 5.1. Payment per man-day from work in the collective farm in the richest Kolkhoz is about three-quarters above that in the poorest of the five. The difference in earnings per worker is even greater due to the greater average intensity of employment in the richer farms. The difference further widens in terms of per capita collective income because the richer farms are able to employ or attract a higher proportion of the available family labour. The difference in terms of per capita income from all sources is smaller because earnings from non-Kolkhoz employment and personal plots exert strong equalising influence.

For the Central Asian region as a whole the difference in average earnings and incomes is likely to be greater among the collective farms. In Uzbekistan payment per man-day in an average Kolkhoz in 1976 was 4.96 rubles. The lowest such payment in any Kolkhoz was reported to be 3.50 rubles while the highest known rate was 11.00 rubles, the ratio of the highest to the lowest being 3.14.[1]

Another way of indirectly measuring inequality among collective farms is to look at the differential in productivity. Table 5.2 shows the distribution of the Uzbek Kolkhoz

TABLE 5.1: Earnings and Incomes in Five Collective Farms

(rubles)

Name of the Kolkhoz	Average Payment per Man-Day	Average Annual Earning from Collective Labour	Per Capita Annual Income from Collective Labour	Per Capita Annual Income from Personal Plot	Per Capita Annual Earning from Outside Employment	Per Capita Total Annual Income
Leninism	7.00	1287	386	102	81	569
Kholkabad	6.15	1187	321	103	118	542
Karl Marx	5.49	783	237	137	89	463
XXII Party Congress	4.07	721	170	138	87	395
Rossiya	4.02	681	69	155	168	392

Note: These data have been reproduced or calculated from Table 6.1 in Chapter 6. The last column includes income from Kolkhoz labour, outside employment and personal plots.

according to the yield of cotton which is frequently the major determinant of collective income. Unfortunately, the size distribution of Kolkhoz is not shown and the highest class interval (3.5 tons per hectare and above) is too large to permit an approximation of something like the comparison between the top and bottom deciles. But it is quite clear that differences are substantial.

Not enough quantitative information is available to analyse the impact of state policy on inter-Kolkhoz income differentials. But, on the whole, such policies may have reduced such inequality. There are at least three instruments which have substantially promoted this objective. The first of these is the procurement price which has been regionally varied to even out the "differential rent" (and perhaps a part of the cost advantage due to the favourable endowment of other resources) in the regions with more favourable conditions and to compensate for the cost disadvantage of the regions with unfavourable conditions. This point was discussed in Chapter 4.

TABLE 5.2: Distribution of Uzbek Kolkhoz According to the Yield of Cotton (tons per hectare), 1976

Yield	Percentage of Kolkhoz
Below 2.0	0.9
2.0–2.5	7.3
2.5–3.0	21.8
3.0–3.5	34.0
3.5 and above	36.0

Source: *NKUz.60*

The details of the operation of the system of taxation are not available but it is known that the collective farms with low profits (below 15 per cent) are exempted from taxation. Thus of the five collective farms for which detailed information is available Kolkhoz XXII Party Congress paid no tax in 1976 due to its low profits.[2]

The final instrument in equalising income among collectives is the contribution of the state to the collective consumption and pension of the Kolkhozniki. These contributions are distributed far more equally than the incomes of the collectives are.

(b) INTRA-KOLKHOZ INEQUALITY

Each Kolkhoz has guaranteed minimum pay. For 25 days' work such pay in most Kolkhoz is 70 rubles per month although in some it is only 60 rubles. Since not all Kolkhozniki work a minimum of 25 days in collective projects the *actual* minimum payment per month may be less than this guaranteed minimum. But those who work fewer than 25 days a month on the farm are usually able to find work for the remaining days, frequently at a wage higher than the minimum guaranteed by the Kolkhoz.[3] Thus, in effect, no Kolkhoznik appears to receive a money income which is less than the guaranteed minimum. Such an income is probably adequate in most cases to secure the basic human needs once it is taken into account that the unfavourable dependency ratio (one worker for 2.5 to 3 members) is partly compensated for by the payment of family allowances (described later) and the provision of low-cost housing, health and education by the Kolkhoz and the state and that the personal plots add a good deal to the income of the family.

It is difficult to arrive at generalisations about differences in income among various categories of employees of a Kolkhoz. Even among the five collective farms studied, there is a considerable difference in the pattern.

One may distinguish three different categories of Kolkhoz employees. At the top are the chairman, the members of the Kolkhoz Board and the specialists like Chief Agronomist, Chief Economist and Chief Book-keeper (some of these specialists are members of the Kolkhoz Board). These employees are on a fixed monthly salary. In the middle category belong the technically skilled workers like tractor drivers. In terms of income the middle level officials—ordinary economists and agronomists and the brigadiers, for example—appear to be at the same level although these officials, unlike skilled workers, are paid fixed monthly incomes. At the bottom are the 'field workers', the production workers with little or no specialised skill. These workers are all paid on the basis of piece-rate work.

Nothing much is known about the dispersion of earnings among the field workers. It is known, however, that there are six grades of such workers and that there are significant differences among the grades. Some idea of the difference is conveyed by the fact that the *average* earning of a field worker is about twice as high as the *minimum* earning (see Table 6.1 in Chapter 6).

In the three Tajik collective farms the earnings of one belonging to the middle category—a tractor driver or a brigadier—are one and three quarters to twice as high as that of a fully employed field worker. The ratio appears to be much lower in the two Uzbek collective farms.

The chief specialists are relatively highly paid. The chairman, frequently himself a specialist, is the only official who receives a salary higher than that of the chief specialists. The chief specialists are paid more than twice as much as a *fully employed* field worker. The chairman's salary is three to four times that of a *fully employed* field worker. But the true income of a chairman is not fully reflected in the salary. Frequently he or she would be provided with a rent-free house of generous proportions and, in the case of the more prosperous collectives, personal cars. In some of the collectives for which the authors collected detailed information such privileges were also accorded the chief specialists.

On the whole, one is left with the impression that there is considerable, but not excessive, inequality in the distribution of earnings. Indeed, it is frequently admitted in discussions that differences in remuneration are kept sufficiently large to promote incentives.

(c) PERSONAL PLOTS AND INCOME DISTRIBUTION

Within a Kolkhoz incomes from personal plots must be fairly equitably distributed. This is because the size of the personal plots is determined on the criterion of roughly the same allocation per *person*. Thus the system may be compared with one of peasant farming with an absolutely egalitarian per capita distribution of land, a ban on the hiring of labour and a compulsory quota on each household for collective labour. It is not surprising that the resulting distribution of income is highly egalitarian, although complete equality is ruled out by the inter-family differences with respect to quality and quantity of labour available to work on personal plots.

Between collective farms, as we have already observed on the basis of our small 'sample' of five, the rank correlation of per capita earnings from personal plots is almost perfectly negatively correlated with per capita collective income. If this phenomenon is representative of that in the region as a whole, then the contribution of the personal plots to inter-Kolkhoz income distribution would be one of equalisation. There are reasons to suggest that this, indeed, is the case. There is very limited variation in the average size of personal plots among the collective farms. The range of feasible technologies would also be limited in view of the very small size of the plots. The lower the return from collective labour, the greater will be the incentive to work the personal plots intensively. All these factors would tend to combine to make the effect of personal plots an equalising one as far as the inter-Kolkhoz distribution is concerned.

Does the result that the distribution of income in the non-socialised part of the Kolkhoz is possibly more egalitarian than in the socialised part sound paradoxical? The distribution of income in the socialised sector, *in principle*, is proportional to the individual member's capacity to work. Individuals differ in terms of such capacity. In the socialised sector such differences in capacity result in larger income differentials because individuals work with relatively large amounts of capital and other resources. Thus the resulting distribution can be as unequal as individuals are in terms of ability.

In the non-socialised sector there are such severe limitations on the volume of means of production per person that the differences among individuals' capacity to work cannot be fully translated into differential results of work. As a consequence, the distribution of income can be less unequal than that of the ability to work. Thus, there is no reason to believe that the result surmised by us on the basis of highly inadequate evidence is unexpected. What must be noted is that the equalising influence of earnings from personal plots is due to the strictly egalitarian limitation on the size of such plots – a limitation that is due to the preponderance of the socialisation of means of production in the economy.

3. SOCIAL CONSUMPTION

In Uzbekistan, the largest Central Asian republic, the per capita payment from social consumption fund (SCF) is approximately 30 per cent of per capita national income (see Chapter 2). Although separate data for the rural areas are not available, it appears that the ratio resulting in such areas is not vastly different. In recent years the SCF has been rising as proportion of national income and personal consumption. The great bulk of the SCFs is financed by the state and the share financed by the Kolkhoz is small, perhaps no greater than 20 per cent on the average. The SCFs at the Kolkhoz level can be divided into two broad types: (i) those held in common by all the collective farms to finance social security common to all Kolkhozy and (ii) those at the disposal of individual collective farms to be used in a more flexible manner to finance the collective consumption needs of their members.

In a number of areas the Kolkhoz supplements the social services provided by the state. Expenditures on education, health and welfare accounted for the following percentages of values-added in the five Kolkhozy visited by the authors:

Karl Marx	6.8
Rossiya	7.2
XXII Party Congress	4.8
Leninism	4.1
Kholkabad	8.9

(See Chapter 6 for further discussion and Table 6.1 for the data.)

Apart from its contribution to social security for its members, the Kolkhoz supplements the state efforts in education and culture. It operates libraries, clubs, and 'palaces of culture' which have facilities for concerts, plays and dances. While the state pays for the operation of the primary and secondary schools, the kindergartens and nursery schools are generally financed by the Kolkhozy. Even in the domain of higher education, where state bursaries and stipends are available for qualified students, the Kolkhozy earmark substantial sums for the students sponsored by them. Some figures on the number of pensioners and students supported by three of the Kolkhozy visited by the authors are given below:

	Total No. of Workers	Pensioners, Invalids, etc.	Sponsored Students
Karl Marx	6346	1483	483
Rossiya	3364	813	221
XXII Party Congress	4048	1799	743

The state and collective farms provide extensive benefits to families in the form of pre-school facilities, children's allowances and benefits for mothers. A wide network of kindergartens and nursery schools is an impressive feature.[4] Without this network it would have been impossible to reach the high levels of female participation in Central Asia where the number of children per family is very high.

Families with young or a large number of children are entitled to additional benefits. Those with a per capita income of less than 50 rubles per month receive 12 rubles per month per child under eight years of age. Those with more than four children are entitled to these allowances irrespective of their income. All women on maternity leave, which extends to 112 days, receive full wages and have their seniority and promotion protected.

6 A Profile of the Five Collective Farms

1. SIZE

In the preceding chapters a good deal of discussion has been based on the data gathered from the five collective farms that the authors visited. It may be useful to discuss in some detail the basic features of the organisation and working of these collective farms to get some idea of how the system works with respect to the aspects about which we have included little or no discussion in the preceding chapters and to see the extent to which the five farms are representative of Central Asian collective agriculture. The first five columns of Table 6.1 give information about these five collective farms. Column 6 shows the average for the five. The remaining three columns show the corresponding averages, where they were available, respectively for Uzbekistan, Tajikistan and USSR.

In terms of household membership an average Uzbek or Tajik Kolkhoz is more than three-quarters bigger than an average Kolkhoz in the USSR. The five collective farms are in turn about three-quarters bigger on the average than the Central Asian collective farms.

An average household in these Kolkhozy has 6.77 members. This is higher than the size of an average rural household in the Indian subcontinent. We do not have the corresponding figures for the Central Asian republics, but, in view of the exceptionally high birth and population growth rates, they are likely to be as high.

2. EMPLOYMENT CHARACTERISTICS

The employment characteristics are worth noting. On the average a third of the employment of the members of the

Kolkhoz households is provided outside the Kolkhoz. The average has been too strongly influenced by the very high ratio of non-Kolkhoz employment in Kolkhoz Rossiya which is located on the outskirts of the city of Dushanbe, the capital of Tajikistan. But even for the other four Kolkhozy the average is nearly a quarter. In the remotely located Kolkhoz Kholkabad 23 per cent of employment is provided by non-Kolkhoz employers. An interesting point to note is that among the five Kolkhozy there is a perfect negative rank correlation between the proportion of employment outside Kolkhoz and the payment per man-day in the Kolkhoz.

The average number of man-days worked per Kolkhoznik is surprisingly low – only 166. For the two republics and for the USSR as a whole the average is approximately 250. This leads us to suspect that there is a considerable overlap between those 'working in Kolkhoz' and those 'working outside Kolkhoz'. It is probable that in the former category those who ever worked in the Kolkhoz during the year have been included and similarly in the latter category. This is why we have converted the number of earners per household working within Kolkhoz into standard employment intensity (250 days per year). If we do the same to the non-Kolkhoz employment[1] and add the two then it is found that an average family of 6.77 has 1.58 fully employed earners. This gives a dependency ratio of 4.3 (counting the earner himself among the dependants) per earner which largely expresses the staggering effect of rapid population growth on the age structure of population.

Female participation in Kolkhoz labour is very high – on the average 48 per cent of the workers in the five Kolkhoz are women. On the other hand, the intensity of female employment, measured as the number of days worked in a year, is much lower than that of men. This must be due largely to the high birth rate with the associated factors such as frequent confinement and a large number of infants to look after. Indeed, the overall figures must be regarded as signifying remarkable achievements in view of these factors and must be attributed to sensible institutions such as universal and communally financed kindergartens.

3. RESOURCE ENDOWMENT

In terms of the land to man ratio these five collective farms appear at first to be at a disadvantage as compared with the average for the two Central Asian republics. But the ratio of land to 'fully employed labour' (i.e., per 250 man-days of labour) is 1.79 hectares which is no lower than the corresponding figure for the republics. Compared to the average for the USSR as a whole the land to man ratio in these Kolkhozy is only about a quarter. The average size of the personal plot in these farms is marginally higher than that for the republics. Compared with the USSR the disadvantage in terms of the size of the personal plot is lower than that in terms of collective land; the average size of the personal plot in these Kolkhoz, as in the republics, is about 40 per cent of that in the USSR.

In terms of capital equipment per unit of land the endowment of the five farms is roughly the same as that for the two Central Asian republics and much greater than that for the USSR as a whole. This is particularly true of tractors for which the relevant data have been presented in the table. For harvesters the variation between the farms is very great, but the overall patterns are similar.

4. PRODUCTION AND PRICING OF COTTON

On the average the five Kolkhozy allocated 55 per cent of their collective land to cotton. This is not very different from the average for the republics. Yield per hectare is a little higher than in the republics.

There is a two-tier system of procurement pricing – a basic price for the given quota that the collectives are expected to fulfil and a 50 per cent premium on the quantity that a Kolkhoz voluntarily sells to the state in excess of the quota.[2] As already noted, the basic price differs between regions within each republic to siphon off the regional differences in cost arising out of the regional differences with respect to factors such as the quality of land. However, the differences in the basic price in the five Kolkhoz must be due largely to the differences in average quality of the cotton as all these collective farms were located in regions which are roughly similar with respect to these factors.

One interesting fact is that the unweighted average rate of premia (calculated as the percentage by which the *average* price of the entire sale above quota exceeds the basic price) is greater than 50 per cent, often by a very big margin. This could be due to a systematically greater over-fulfilment of the quota for the superior qualities. This may indicate that the prices for different qualities are set in a way that profitability is greater for the superior qualities.

The system of incentive payment does not consist of the simple payment of a 50 per cent premium. There are provisions for additional payments for timely delivery and for the degree of mechanisation in certain operations. It was not possible to obtain a complete picture of the system of such payments, but it was clear that part of the explanation for the unweighted average rate of premia being above 50 per cent may lie in these numerous complex provisions.

It was not possible to ascertain the detailed criteria for the fixation of quota. The ratio of excess quota sale differs greatly even among the five Kolkhozy – from only 15 per cent to as much as 61 per cent. A lower quota in relation to the production possibility would indicate a lower rate of implicit tax or a higher rate of implicit subsidy. It was impossible to find out how the procurement authorities set quota in relation to the production possibilities in different Kolkhozy so as to make the system reasonably equitable. If the recent average output is the basis then the system would punish efficiency. It is possible that some regional norms of productivity are used to determine such quota. Such a practice would provide sufficient incentive to the individual farms to exceed the norm and earn higher income on the excess output. It was not possible to ascertain what happens if a Kolkhoz fails to fulfil a quota. In *principle* a quota is fixed through a voluntary contract between Kolkhoz and the procurement authorities.

5. INCOME AND EARNINGS

The payment per man-day in the five collective farms was significantly higher than that in the republics. This points to the fact that, on the average, these farms are more prosperous than an average Central Asian Kolkhoz. But these farms differed very widely in terms of such prosperity. Two of the Tajik collective farms were significantly below the regional and Tajik averages in terms of payment per man-day.

The table shows that the average *annual* earning per Kolkhoznik from collective agriculture is lower in these farms as compared with the averages for the republic. As already noted, this is due to the lower intensity of Kolkhoz employment per Kolkhoznik that was observed in these farms. Once these earnings are converted into that per 'fully employed Kolkhoznik' the advantage that these farms have over their average Central Asian counterparts would become clear.

In the table three sources of average annual family income have been shown in the following order: collective Kolkhoz labour, personal plots and non-Kolkhoz employment. Our confidence in these data has the same ordering. Although an attempt was made to estimate earnings from personal plots at market value (i.e., by converting the self-consumed quantity at the Kolkhoz market price rather than at procurement price), the extent to which it succeeded is not known. For non-Kolkhoz employment a daily wage rate which is 20 per cent above the payment in the Kolkhoz was used. This seemed to be a reasonable order of magnitude on the basis of what was found out about the relative urban-rural wage rates in the relevant localities. But the uniform application of this ratio, irrespective of the season, type and location of non-Kolkhoz labour, must have resulted in some error.

The average shares of the three sources in the aggregate family income of the five collective farms are as follows:

Collective Kolkhoz labour	47 per cent
Personal plots	29 per cent
Non-Kolkhoz employment	24 per cent

But the shares vary a great deal among the farms. As already noted, there is nearly perfect inverse rank correlation between collective earning and earning from personal plot. The inverse association between earning from non-Kolkhoz employment and collective earning is almost as strong.

6. OTHER ASPECTS

The saving-investment behaviour, the comparison of income scales for various categories of employees and the comparative return per hectare from personal and collective agriculture in the five farms have been discussed in some detail in the preceding chapters.

Expenditure on education, health and welfare amounts to 6.6 per cent of value added on the average. The bulk of the current payment for these services at the Kolkhoz is borne by the state. It is clear that the Kolkhoz spending per capita on these items varies a great deal from one Kolkhoz to another in our small list. This may appear to be in conflict with the observation that the levels of these services are not too dissimilar between different Kolkhozy. The explanation is that these expenditures include capital constructions such as hospital and school buildings. In a given year expenditure on such items can vary greatly among collectives.

All the five collective farms have two-tiered organisation structures consisting of the Kolkhoz at the top and the brigade at the bottom. None had zvenos which sometimes form the lowest tier of a three-tiered structure elsewhere in the USSR.[3] On the average, a Kolkhoz has 30 brigades and the average number of workers per brigade is 81 which seems somewhat high for the efficient enforcement of work discipline and an accurate evaluation of work performance.

TABLE 6.1: A Profile of Five Soviet Central Asian Collective Farms with Some Comparative Data for the Republics and all USSR

	Karl Marx (Tajikistan)	Rossiya (Tajikistan)	XXII Party Congress (Tajikistan)	Leninism (Uzbekistan)	Kholkabad (Uzbekistan)	Average of the five Kolkhoz	Average for all Kolkhoz in Uzbekistan 1976	Average for all Kolkhoz in Tajikistan 1973	Average for all Kolkhoz in USSR 1976
No. of households	2338	1420	1891	854	1045	1510	866	861	486
Average size of a household	6.84	7.75	6.35	5.90	6.77	6.77	–	–	–
Total no. of workers:									
Working in Kolkhoz	4833	1104	2838	1515	1911	2440	1110	1027	534
Working outside Kolkhoz	1513	2260	1210	265	587	1167	–	–	–
No. of earners per household:									
Working in Kolkhoz	2.07	0.78	1.50	1.77	1.83	1.61	–	–	–
Working outside	0.65	1.59	0.64	0.31	0.56	0.77	–	–	–
Total	2.72	2.37	2.14	2.08	2.39	2.38	–	–	–
No. of earners per household in standard employment intensity (250 man-days per year):									
Working in Kolkhoz	1.18	0.53	1.06	1.30	1.41	1.07	–	–	–
Female workers as per cent of total workers in Kolkhoz	48.8	44.4	43.1	56.2	51.8	48.0	–	–	–

Average No. of man-days worked by a Kolkhoz worker:	142.6	169.4	177.2	183.8	193.0	166.3	252.6	251.8	247.9
(male)	–	–	–	(215.9)	(202.2)	–	–	–	–
(female)	–	–	–	(158.9)	(184.5)	–	–	–	–
Area of collective sown land[1] (hectares)	3736	1400	3639	2617	3152	2909	1777	1950	3539
Area under personal plots (ha)[2]	309	240	245	146	128	214	97500	27100	4300,000
Collective land per Kolkhoz worker (in ha)	0.77	1.27	1.28	1.73	1.65	1.19	1.60	1.90	6.63
Average personal plot per household (in ha)	0.13	0.17	0.13	0.17	0.12	0.14	0.12	0.13	0.33
Hectares of total sown land: per household	1.73	1.15	2.05	3.24	3.14	2.06	2.17	2.39	7.61
per person	0.25	0.15	0.32	0.55	0.46	0.30	–	–	–
Per cent of collective land under cotton	60.4	43.0	41.8	45.9	76.2	54.9	63.3	40.0	–
Cotton yield (raw cotton, ton/hectare)	3.44	3.25	3.24	4.30	3.14	3.42	3.30	3.08	–
Average basic procurement price per ton of raw cotton (rubles)	660.08	430.69	482.72	492.1	502.92	564.09	–	–	–
Realised 'premia' per ton as per cent of basic procurement price (unweighted average for all qualities)	68.6	77.4	52.7	58.8	101.6	62.7	–	–	–
Per cent of collective land under grain	–	30.0	26.9	19.0	23.8	18.2	17.4	39.6	57.2

TABLE 6.1: (continued)

	Karl Marx (Tajikistan)	Rossiya (Tajikistan)	XXII Party Congress (Tajikistan)	Leninism (Uzbekistan)	Kholkabad (Uzbekistan)	Average of the five Kolkhoz	Average for all Kolkhoz in Uzbekistan 1976	Average for all Kolkhoz in Tajikistan 1973	Average for all Kolkhoz in USSR 1976
Grain yield (ton/hectare)	–	1.28	1.59	1.42	1.84	1.58	1.69	1.14	1.75
Hectares of collective sown land per tractor	23	30	21	29	18	22.3	21	29	92
No. of cattle:	2000	1300	3567	909	2360	2027	835	1288	1722
including milk cows	604	300	930	300	545	536	226	351	568
No. of sheep and goats	...	5900	...	1491	...	1478	1307	4500	1842
Average payment per man-day (rubles)	5.49	4.02	4.07	7.00	6.15	5.33	4.96	4.37	4.77
Average annual earning per worker from collective Kolkhoz labour (at actual intensity of employment) (male)	783	681	721	1287	1187	885	1253	1100	1183
(female)[3]	–	–	–	1511	1244	–	–	–	–
				1112	1135				
Average annual family income from collective Kolkhoz labour	1621	531	1082	2277	2172	1426	–	–	–
Average annual income from personal plot per family[4]	936	1200	878	600	700	900	–	–	–

Average family earning from outside employment[5]	611	1299	554	479	798	737	—	—	—
Total household income from above three sources	3167.3	3030.5	2513.7	3355.9	3669.9	3063	—	—	—
Per capita income from above three sources	463.1	391.0	395.9	568.8	542.1	452.4	—	—	—
Gross money income (thousand rubles)	6528	1527	4247	3998	5508	4362	—	—	—
Current inputs, amortisation, etc. (thousand rubles)	1331	423	1852	1178	1363	1229	—	—	—
Value added in collective production (thousand rubles)	5197	1104	2395	2820	4145	3133	2058[6]	1714[6]	846[6]
Per cent of value added allocated to:									
Labour payment	73	68	85	69	55	69	64	66	76
Investment (financed by internal saving)	16.4	23.3	9.9	21.8	18.0	17.3	—	—	—
Education, health, welfare	6.8	7.2	4.8	4.1	8.9	6.6	—	—	—
Tax	4.0	1.4	...	5.2	6.6	4.1	—	—	—
Reserve fund etc.	—	—	—	—	11.7	3.1	—	—	—
Investment financed by long-term borrowing as per cent of value added	...	18.0	3.9	10.6	...	3.8	—	—	—
Total investment as per cent of value added	16.4	41.3	13.8	32.4	18.0	21.1	—	—	—
Total internal saving as per cent of value added	16.4	23.3	9.9	21.8	29.7	20.4	—	—	—

TABLE 6.1: *(continued)*

	Karl Marx (Tajikistan)	Rossiya (Tajikistan)	XXII Party Congress (Tajikistan)	Leninism (Uzbekistan)	Kholkabad (Uzbekistan)	Average of the five Kolkhoz	Average for all Kolkhoz in Uzbekistan 1976	Average for all Kolkhoz in Tajikistan 1973	Average for all Kolkhoz in USSR 1976
Gross value of output (rubles) per sown hectare of collective agriculture	1747	1091	1167	1528	1747	1499	–	–	–
Gross value of output (rubles) per hectare of personal plot[7]	7200	7059	6754	3529	5833	6364	–	–	–
Output per hectare of personal plot as the ratio of that for collective land	4.1	6.5	5.8	2.3	3.3	4.25	–	–	–
No. of brigades (including firma)	47	21	37	18	27	30	–	–	–
Average no. of workers per brigade	103	53	77	84	71	81	–	–	–
Monthly average earnings (rubles) of:									
Chairman	500	300	412	500	480	438	–	–	–
Chief book-keeper/Chief economist	–	–	–	315	380	348 (U)	–	–	–
Brigadier	300	175	170	280	173	220 (U)	–	–	–

Tractor driver	350	245	180	260	175	242 (U)	–	–	–
Average worker (for average no. of days worked)	65	57	60	107	99	78 (U)	–	–	–
Minimum guaranteed income (at the rate of working of an average worker)[8]	29	40	36	43	45	39 (U)	–	–	–
Average worker for 25 days' work in a month	137	101	102	175	154	134 (U)	–	–	–
Minimum guaranteed income for 25 days' work in a month	60	70	60	70	70	–	–	–	–

Notes:
1. Sown area refers to land under crops, orchards and vineyards.
2. Personal plot includes total area under such plots. Sown area under personal plots is 85 per cent of total in Uzbekistan, 89 per cent of total in Tajikistan and 84 per cent for all USSR.
3. Female earnings are calculated on the assumption that the distributions of labour force among categories earning different rates of income are the same for male and female. This assumption is almost certainly inaccurate – the differential between sexes is, therefore, greater than is estimated here.
4. Personal plot earnings are estimated at market prices. Where estimates were given by the responding Kolkhoz at state prices a 30 per cent mark up was added.
5. It is assumed that daily earning per worker outside the Kolkhoz is 20 per cent higher than that in the Kholkhoz.
6. From the statistical reports it is not quite clear if these are gross values of output or values added. We think they refer to the latter.
7. Value of output per hectare of personal plot refers to total, not just sown, land. To convert these into values per hectare of sown land a multiplier of 1.18 for Uzbekistan and 1.12 for Tajikistan should be used.
8. The lowest minimum guaranteed monthly income (frequently 70 rubles, but sometimes 60 rubles) is paid for 25 days of work per month. Our figures are proportionate to average number of days worked.
9. The entries in the column 'Average of the Five Kolkhoz' usually show weighted averages. Those which are not so have been marked (U), meaning unweighted.
10. – means not available or not shown and . . . means zero.
11. Sources for the Uzbek, Tajik and all USSR. figures are usually: *Narodnoe Khozyaistvo Uzbekskoi SSR Za 60 Let. Sovietski Tajikistan Za 50 Let* and *Narodnoe Khozyaistvo SSSR Za 60 Let.*

7 Some Concluding Observations

The Soviet Central Asian republics constituted a backward and poor region as recently as four decades ago with a living standard not qualitatively different from that of its immediate neighbours – Afghanistan, for example. Within a relatively short period these republics achieved a remarkable transformation. By 1976 per capita income in Uzbekistan, the largest of the republics, was above current US$1300 at the official rate of exchange. Income per head for the region as a whole was not much different. Even recognising the problems of the rate of exchange and the differences in the method of accounting, one is led by such figures to conclude that the living standard in Central Asia today is incomparably superior to that of most of its Asian neighbours. In the comparison of the provisions of collective consumption and social services the Soviet Central Asian republics stand out even more clearly.

The transformation in Central Asia has taken place during a period of high and accelerating rate of growth in population. The high population growth not only raised the required rate of growth in overall income for a given rate of growth in per capita income but also raised the dependency ratio and made it necessary to devote a greater proportion of resources to education, child care and certain related services.

The attainment of prosperity in the Central Asian republics has not come through the classical path of industrialisation. The industrial progress of the region has no doubt been very substantial, but rapid growth in agriculture has been a key element in their progress. A distinctive and related feature of their experience has been the continued predominance of the rural sector. While the region was not behind (and indeed Uzbekistan, the leading republic, was ahead of) the rest of the

102

USSR in terms of urbanisation immediately before the revolution, by now the region continues to be predominantly rural and behind the rest of the USSR in terms of urbanisation. The lower rate of urbanisation has not meant a lower rate of growth: the phenomenon was not the well-known one of stagnation and failure to industrialise. What the Central Asian republics experienced was rapid agricultural growth leading to a rising standard of living in the rural areas and the consequent absence of pressure to move out of the rural society. The rising living standard in the rural areas also made it possible to keep the urban-rural income differential low – a factor which weakened the pull of the urban areas. Thus Central Asia experienced economic development with rural development and in this sense deserves to be studied carefully by those countries which cannot hope to develop by classical type of industrialisation.

The chief element of the material progress of agriculture was a specialisation in cotton characterised by a very high rate of increase in yield per hectare. Starting from a low level the region soon surpassed all significant producers of cotton in the world in terms of output per hectare at the same time that its agriculture became increasingly specialised in cotton.

The specialisation and prosperity in cotton were brought about by providing very high price incentives. While collectivised agriculture in much of the rest of the USSR was subjected to a high rate of accumulation and resource transfer through the adoption of what came to be known as the policy of 'primitive socialist accumulation' cotton, the main marketed produce of Central Asian agriculture, was not subjected to similarly adverse terms of trade. For the two decades starting in the mid 1930s, cotton enjoyed extraordinarily favourable terms of trade in comparison with other major products of Soviet agriculture. As a result Central Asia became increasingly more specialised in cotton and its agricultural income increased very rapidly.

The truly remarkable nature of the Central Asian agricultural growth gets fully revealed only in the context of the vast institutional change that preceded it – the kind of institutional change that is known frequently to have produced at least temporary disruptions in output elsewhere. In less than a decade Central Asia experienced a transition from backward feudal relations to institutions like collective and state farms with only a very brief interregnum during which private peasant ownership existed. Nor is it known that the rural population had undergone a long political struggle which would have prepared them ideologically for collectivisation. And yet these institutions did not prove so difficult to adapt to as to prevent rapid growth in output. A proper and complete explanation of the phenomenon is beyond the scope of the present study. However, available evidence suggests that production gains did not immediately follow collectivisation. There was a period of hesitation and decline in yield until policies towards agriculture changed from the one of discrimination to encouragement through incentives. The exceptional experience of Central Asia probably constitutes the evidence that successful institution of advanced forms of organisation such as the collectives can be achieved only if the overall policies are sensible enough to provide appropriate incentives and rewards. That so many experiences of collective agriculture in the last half century have failed to serve as vehicles of agricultural growth is probably more due to inappropriate overall policies towards agriculture than to any inherent difficulties.

The experience of the last quarter century underlines the importance of flexibility in organisation to changing economic environment brought about by rapid growth and increasing complexity in the production system. Thus, alongside with the economic reforms affecting other forms of productive enterprises the collective farms have benefited since the early 1950s from growing autonomy in production planning and from the substitution of indirect for more direct methods of state control.

The collective farms have been the main forms of organisation in Central Asian agriculture. Over the years the state farms have increased their share of total farm households, but to this day the collective farms cover nearly three quarters more of the farm households than do the state farms. Compared with the rest of the USSR the agriculture in Central Asia has a greater preponderance of the collective farms. While no conclusive generalisations can be made on the

question, available evidence provides no basis for the conclusion that the performance of an average collective farm has
been inferior to that of an average state farm. Indeed, under
certain plausible assumptions about relative factor scarcities,
one might be tempted to conclude that the opposite was true.

The collective agriculture has facilitated growth with a
relatively egalitarian income distribution. Poverty entailing
hunger, disease and lack of clothing and shelter is unknown.
The relative egalitarianism in the distribution of income has
been reinforced further by the provision of social consumption
which is perhaps even more equally distributed. The state plays
a key role in this sphere but its efforts are supplemented in
several directions by the collective farms. Social consumption
has formed a rising proportion of the aggregate income of
collective farms. In addition to education, health and cultural
facilities, major strides have also been made in recent years in
the field of social security and family benefits. This policy of
collective provision of goods and services played an important
role in meeting the basic human needs of the masses.

All this is not to deny the existence of significant inequalities
in the distribution of *earnings*. The spread between real
earnings of the top management and the earnings of the field
workers would appear quite large. Similarly, the skill differentials seem to be considerable. Such differentials are officially
justified by the need to provide material incentives for work
and higher productivity. Unfortunately, it has been impossible
for the present writers to assemble any comprehensive
measurement of income distribution on the basis of which
comparisons with other systems might be attempted.

While the productivity achievements of the system have
been truly remarkable in terms of output per hectare of land
(which, contrary to the impression of the vast expanse of
territory, is a relatively scarce factor) the output per worker
continues to be very low compared to the agriculture in the
advanced countries. There are also some important questions
concerning the efficiency of utilisation of scarce capital inputs
like tractors. For further material progress the collective
agriculture of Central Asia must face up to these problems and
challenges.

Notes

CHAPTER 1

1. Administratively each republic is divided into a number of *Oblasts* (provinces) which in turn are divided into *Raions* (districts). Sometimes a republic contains one or more Autonomous Soviet Socialist Republics (ASSRs), each of them consisting of a separate nationality that deserves special status. Sometimes Oblasts are also accorded autonomous status. There are fifteen republics in the Union of Soviet Socialist Republics (USSR).
2. In 1970 the proportion of Russians in total population was 12.5 per cent in Uzbekistan and 11.9 per cent in Tajikistan.
3. Thus the present day population of Uzbekistan, the biggest of the four republics, consists of more than 100 nationalities of which the following are prominent: Uzbeks (64.7 per cent), Russians (12.5 per cent), Tatars (4.8 per cent), Kazakhs (4.6 per cent) and Tajiks (3.8 per cent).
4. The official names of the republics are the Soviet Socialist Republics (SSRs). As already stated, an SSR may contain Autonomous Soviet Socialist Republics (ASSRs) within its boundaries as special administrative regions and sometimes *Oblasts* (provinces) are given autonomous status (as was Kara-Kirghiz between 1924 and 1926 and Karakalpak between 1924 and 1932).

CHAPTER 2

1. One should qualify such comparisons with reference to the point that the lower death rate in Soviet Central Asia is partly due to its young age structure.
2. Tajikistan, Uzbekistan, Turkmenistan and Kirghizia (in that order) have the highest ranks among the 15 Soviet republics in terms of birth rate and population growth.
3. One could argue that the same conditions prevailed elsewhere in the USSR. To the extent that this was the case the higher birth rate in Central Asia must be explained by different tradition and culture (which leads to a different perception of these objective conditions). The predominance of rural life is probably an important factor.
4. It should be noted that any such comparison should allow for the fact that women as a proportion of total population are greater for the USSR as a whole (53.5 per cent in recent years) than for Central Asia (51 per

cent in Tajikistan in 1970). But this difference cannot explain the large difference in the proportion of women as members of the labour force.

5. As explained in the footnote to Table 2.5 these workers do not make up the entire labour force. However, they virtually represent the entire civilian labour force. It is possible, but not obvious, that a comparison of the more complete estimates of labour force would give a somewhat lower difference in workers per 100 persons between the USSR and the Central Asian republics.

6. Latvia, which became a part of the USSR much later, was another exception.

7. The following information is available on the basis of the 1959 Census: (a) In Tashkent, the capital of Uzbekistan, Russians (44 per cent of the population) outnumbered the Uzbeks (34 per cent); (b) Tajiks formed only 31 per cent of the urban population of Tajikistan while they accounted for 82 per cent of the total population of the republic; (c) the Slav population outnumbered the native population in Frunze, the capital of Kirghizia. These figures are quoted in Violet Conolly, *Beyond the Urals* (London: Oxford University Press, 1967), p. 111.

8. One may wonder if a discussion of such factors is of any relevance in view of the widely held belief that the Soviet authorities determine the location of population by physical control. What we are suggesting is that the underlying incentive pattern was not too inconsistent with whatever physical control the authorities might have, or would have, used. Indeed, it is doubtful if physical controls alone could secure location of population over a long period if incentives were sharply contrary to such controls.

9. These are the rates of growth in the indices of industrial *production* and not of *value added*. To the extent the complexity of production has been increasing over time, without a corresponding increase in the vertical integration of processes within the same enterprise, these rates would overstate the rates of growth in industrial values added. On this and on the general problem of index numbers in the USSR a considerable literature is available. See, for example, Alec Nove, *The Soviet Economy*, George Allen and Unwin, London 1968.

10. As we shall see later, the terms of trade for agriculture improved significantly over the decade. Since the sectoral shares are derived from the current price estimates this means that the decline in the share of agricultural value added *at constant price* was greater than is shown by the figures.

11. It is not very satisfactory to speculate about a trend on the basis of only four observations. But the last two rows of Table 2.7 suggest that the per capita income and consumption disparities between Uzbekistan and the USSR have widened a little between 1965 and 1976. We hope that the discussion in the following pages will make it clear that in our view the disparity in per capita income between Central Asia and the USSR: (a) became reduced gradually over the two decades leading to the mid-1950s and (b) may have increased slightly thereafter.

12. As we shall discuss in detail in later chapters, the two main forms of agricultural organisation in the USSR are Kolkhoz (the collective farm) and Sovkhoz (the state farm). In a collective farm the assets are owned or held collectively by the members who provide labour and share among themselves the net earnings. In a state farm the assets are owned by the state and the labour force is paid wages just as in any industrial enterprise. Over time the proportion of agricultural labour force in the Sovkhoz has been increasing and that in Kolkhoz has been going down. But this process has been slower in Central Asia than in the rest of the USSR. In 1976 the Sovkhoz workers were 37 per cent of the total Kolkhoz and Sovkhoz workers in Uzbekistan as compared to 43 per cent in the USSR. Besides Kolkhoz and Sovkhoz there are some other agricultural enterprises which employ a very small proportion of the agricultural labour force.

13. *Novy Mir*, 10/59 quoted in Alec Nove and J. A. Newth, *The Soviet Middle East* (London: George Allen and Unwin, 1967), p. 103.

14. Thus, let us compare Uzbekistan with the USSR in this regard. In 1970 Kolkhoz payment per day in Uzbekistan was 4.24 rubles and that in the USSR was 3.90 rubles. Sovkhoz payment per day was 4.43 rubles in the USSR and 4.30 rubles in Uzbekistan (assuming that the income ratio of 0.97 in State agriculture applies to Sovkhoz income ratios of Uzbekistan to the USSR). The share of Sovkhoz was 0.35 for the USSR and 0.28 for Uzbekistan. Thus the weighted average agricultural earning was 4.25 rubles per day in Uzbekistan—only 4 per cent above the 4.09 rubles in the USSR. In these calculations it has been assumed that Kolkhoz and Sovkhoz make up all agriculture. Even if allowance is made for the small amount of the other forms of agricultural organisations, the above calculations would remain pretty much unchanged.

15. Thus in 1970 the average number of family members per earning member in a Kolkhoz was 3.93 in Uzbekistan and 2.80 in the USSR as a whole. Therefore, although the earning per day per Kolkhoz worker was 9 per cent higher there, income from Kolkhoz per capita in Uzbekistan was 22 per cent lower than in all USSR.

16. Per capita earnings from personal plots are probably lower in Central Asia than in the rest of the USSR. Average size of the personal plot per household is 2.36 times higher in USSR than in Central Asia where the household size is considerably larger than in the rest of the USSR. See the table on the profile of five Kolkhoz in Chapter 6 for comparative data on the size of personal plots.

17. Excluding payments out of public consumption fund Uzbek per capita consumption in 1976 would be 59.2 per cent of that in the USSR as a whole. Including such payments the ratio increases to 63.7 per cent. Note that while the inclusion of public consumption fund reduces the *geometric* difference, it *increases* the *arithmetic* difference.

18. The Asian and Latin American figures are from Alexander Dorozynski, *Doctors and Healers* (Ottawa: International Development Research Centre, 1975), p. 9.

19. The above discussion relates to educational and health provision per

10,000 population. When account is taken of the relatively much higher rate of population growth in Uzbekistan and Tajikistan, the expansion in absolute terms in educational and health facilities has been quite extraordinary.

20. Perhaps the most cogent statement of the doctrine that was to be implemented later is contained in the writings of E. Preobrazhensky (*The New Economics*, Clarendon, 1965). He forcefully argued, in this book, first published in 1924, that to develop a socialist economy in the Soviet Union, resources must be extracted from the then non-socialist parts of the economy – the petty bourgeois and, above all, the peasantry. He describes the methods of transferring resources from the then private peasantry to the state. Besides considering taxation, profits from foreign trade and borrowing, he proposed the method of 'non-equivalent exchange' as the most powerful instrument to effect such transfer. Such non-equivalent exchange between the town and the country would constitute the manipulation of the prices offered by the state to the peasantry and the prices charged by it on the sale of industrial goods to the peasantry. For an account of this theory and how it became a reality in the Soviet Union a few years after the publication of Preobrazhensky's book see (in addition to Preobrazhensky's own work): M. Lewin, *Russian Peasants and Soviet Power* (London: George Allen and Unwin, 1967) and A. Ehrlich, *The Soviet Industrialisation Debate*, Harvard University Press 1967. Stalin's own account of the justification for the implementation of such a policy is to be found in: J. V. Stalin, 'The Right Deviation in the C.P.S.U. (B)' in *Problems of Leninism* (Moscow: Foreign Languages Publishing House, 1953). What the effect of the policy was in reality is not absolutely clear. It has been claimed that the accumulation from this source was not such a large part of overall capital formation.

21. The fall in output per hectare in the early 1930s must also partly be ascribed to the organisational transition of agriculture in those days.

22. This is the all USSR ratio for 1976. For Central Asia the ratio was lower.

23. Meat, milk, grains and cotton (in that order) are the four biggest items of state procurement in terms of value in recent years and together they account for nearly three-quarters of the total state payments for procurement. In the earlier years the ordering in value terms was different for obvious reasons.

24. It should be mentioned that whether cotton was actually subsidised depends on the appropriateness of the exchange rate. If in 1952 the appropriate exchange rate was such that a ruble should have exchanged for 24 per cent fewer dollars than it officially did then the procurement price on cotton would have been the same as international price at the appropriate exchange rate. Whatever the appropriate exchange rate the rate of concealed taxation (or subsidy) on cotton was way below (above) that on grains and meat. It should be reiterated that what we call 'concealed tax' is the difference between actual income and the income that would accrue if the producers could sell internationally at the going price. One can easily think of reasons why such a situation would be

undesirable for the nation to adopt: adoption would imply acceptance of the existing international specialisation as the optimal solution. There is also no stipulation that the average prices (themselves subject to many errors mentioned above) would remain the same if a major producer/consumer like the USSR were to buy or sell more internationally. In spite of all these qualifications it is quite clear that, however correct or incorrect the interventions were, the effect was asymmetrical on the incomes of the producers of cotton as compared with other agricultural producers.

25. To make this argument there is no need to go so far as to argue that in the absence of the price incentives the state would have failed to achieve an expansion in cotton acreage by other means. The evidence in the preceding section shows, however, that such other means in the 1930s failed to secure an increase in cotton acreage with increasing yield.

26. The trend in labour requirement for sugar beet, potato and vegetables is similar to that for grains. The relative labour intensity of cotton, especially in harvesting, becomes obvious to even a casual observer of the Central Asian rural scene in the autumn. The present authors witnessed a great deal of cotton picking by hand. All the officials emphasised that the target of increasing the share of mechanical picking was a very important one. In some places the present authors were told that there were technical problems of designing harvesters that would pick high quality cotton without waste.

27. These calculations are based on the combination of the income shares shown in *NK SU 60* with the income data for which sources have been shown above. To derive Kolkhoz income for this purpose the actual number of days worked per month (21) has been used. It is possible that this differential may have declined in recent years primarily because of the extension of social security benefits to the Kolkhozniki.

28. Actual figures are not available but in 1970 per capita income from this source in a Kolkhoz in Uzbekistan and Tajikistan were respectively 58 and 37 per cent of the all-Union average. Earnings from collective labour were, as we have seen, a much higher proportion. Source: A. Teryaeva, *Voprosy Economiki*, 1972, No. 5, p. 71.

29. One general comment needs to be made about the prices in Table 2.13. These are the *average* prices; i.e., total value divided by the total quantity procured. Thus some year to year variation is attributable to quality change, changes in regional shares (since prices differ between regions) and similar factors.

30. The cost ratios of cotton to grain in the Central Asian republics are as follows:

Uzbekistan	3.53
Tajikistan	3.62
Kirghizia	5.69
Turkmenistan	4.03

But the grain prices are higher in these republics than in the USSR on the average. We have no information on the grain procurement prices in the republics in 1962, but it is pretty certain that the price to cost ratio in these places had also become more favourable for grain by 1962.

31. A. N. Malafeyev, op cit.

32. V. Khlebnikov, 'O Dal 'neyshem Ukreplenii Ekonomiki Kolkhozov', *Voprosy Economiki*, No. 7 (1962), p. 50. Although cotton lost its privileged position in relation to the other products its price did not decline absolutely. The explanation of the alleged fall in income must, therefore, be sought in rising costs of production. Until 1958 the tractors and agricultural machineries were centralised in the Machine Tractor Stations (MTS) which provided the Kolkhoz with the service of these machines at prices specified by them. In 1958 the MTS were disbanded and their machinery was sold to the Kolkhoz. It has been suggested that the financing of the acquisition of these machines and equipment at unfavourable terms was a main cause of the rising costs and lower labour payments in the years immediately following 1958.

33. As already hinted at, procurement prices differ from one region to another. The main reason for such variation is to cover differences in cost due to differential land rent arising out of differences in land quality. Since the payment of land rent does not exist in the USSR, this device has provided a useful instrument to prevent inequalities of income due to differential rent. The point will be discussed in greater detail later.

34. *NK SU 60*, p. 355. It is not clear how costs are calculated. Presumably labour costs are included. Since labour payment is partly dependent on prices received, the argument that prices are set to cover costs involves an element of circularity.

35. It is needless to repeat that this statement is subject to all the qualifications elaborated at the end of Section 5 of this Chapter.

36. These are the all-USSR indices. From the available information about the prices of individual goods at state retail outlets in the Central Asian republics, it is pretty clear that the trends there are about the same. We are less certain about the trends in the Kolkhoz market prices in the republics.

37. The trend rate of growth in the price index at urban Kolkhoz market (Y) is calculated by fitting the following regression on time (t = time measured in years; 1 for 1950, 5 for 1954 etc.):

$$\log Y = 4.53 + 0.023t, \ R^2 = 0.64.$$

Thus the trend rate of increase in the index of Kolkhoz market prices is 2.3 per cent per year.

38. The R^2 is 0.01 for 17 observations. This means that virtually none of the variation in Y is explained by the variation in X.

39. A billion is equivalent to a thousand millions in this essay.

CHAPTER 3

1. Rakhima Aminova, 'Land-and-Water Reforms in Uzbekistan', in

Izdatee' stvo Fan, Tashkent 1975, p. 354.

2. These were the findings of a survey, reported in Aminova, op cit, of 11,700 households which were given allotments in the second land-and-water reform.

3. Aminova, op cit, reports that after the reforms in Uzbekistan the poor peasants made up 37.6 per cent and middle peasants 61 per cent of the total, while the rich peasants made up only 1.4 per cent of the agricultural households. These categories are not defined. Nor is any information available about the actual size distribution of agricultural landownership before, or after, the reform.

4. Aminova, op cit.

5. A few facts need to be highlighted. First, the acceleration of the pace of collectivisation was a decision initiated and implemented by the central leadership. Secondly, the implementation of the programme was carried out through *ad hoc* bodies mobilised for this purpose – not through the village Soviet administration. Thirdly, the pace of official implementation was frequently out of line with the voluntary decisions of the peasantry. In a way, this last point was officially recognised quite early. In 1930 the leadership urged the party cadres to take greater caution. See J. Stalin's famous article, 'Dizzy with Success' in *Pravda*, 2 March 1930.

6. The Model Rules of 1935 referred to the collective farms as 'artels' which, in the present context, meant a co-operative or a collective.

7. See Douglas Diamond, 'Trends in Outputs, Inputs and Factor Productivity in Soviet Agriculture' in US Government, Joint Economic Committee, *New Directions in the Soviet Economy*, Washington DC, 1966.

8. These quotations are from article 52 of the Charter as translated in *The Current Digest of the Soviet Press*, 13 January 1970.

9. Robert S. Stuart, *The Collective Farm in Soviet Agriculture*, p. 111. (D.C. Heath and Company, 1972). The author, however, indicates that many of these changes in plan methodology were not always implemented in practice.

10. For more details on easier bank credit available to Kolkhozy, see James R. Millar, 'Financing the Modernization of Kolkhozy' in James R. Millar (ed.), *The Soviet Rural Economy* (University of Illinois, 1971). Millar, however, concludes on the basis of the evidence over 1949–62, that the Kolkhozy have made relatively little use of increased financial flexibility. He explains this by reference to the state credit and financial policies. It is possible that his conclusion may be the result of aggregation and that individual Kolkhoz make greater use of credit facilities than indicated in his article. The data we collected on five collective farms in Uzbekistan and Tajikistan indicate considerable use of borrowing to finance investment (see Table 6.1 in Chapter 6).

11. For a detailed discussion, see Stuart, op cit, Chapters 5 and 6.

12. L. I. Brezhnev, *Report of the CPSU Central Committee and the Immediate Tasks of the Party in Home and Foreign Policy* (Moscow, 1976), p. 63.

13. On organisational structure in the Kolkhozy, see S. G. Kolesnev,

'Collective Farms – Socialist Agricultural Enterprises' in L. Kolesnikov (ed.) *Agriculture of the Soviet Union* (Moscow: Mir Publishers, 1970).
14. For details see Table 6.1 in Chapter 6.
15. See, for instance, A. N. Kosygin, *Guidelines for the Development of the National Economy of the USSR for 1976–1980* (Moscow, 1976), p. 64.

CHAPTER 4

1. We recognise that a comparison of efficiency must be based on more general measurement and not on the output per unit of a single factor. But, to arrive at more general measures, we need to quantify relative social scarcities of different factors. On this we have few guidelines either for Central Asia or for the countries with which comparisons are to be made. Later in this chapter we shall try to guess which factors in Central Asia are relatively more scarce and, on that basis, arrive at some tentative judgments on the question of efficiency.
2. The average yield in the collective farms of the republics was about 3.27 tons and that in the five farms 3.42 tons which is 5 per cent higher. The data for the five farms are summarised in Table 6.1 in Chapter 6.
3. For the all Union figures on the degree of tractorisation see *NK SU 60* for the relevant data.
4. The US figures have been calculated from CIA, *USSR Agricultural Atlas*, Washington, DC, 1974.
5. The sources of the data for the USSR and USA are the same as those mentioned in the preceding footnotes. It may be mentioned that in terms of horsepower an average Soviet tractor is bigger than an American one.
6. In some of the collective farms visited by the authors manual harvesting of cotton was widespread. To give an example, Kolkhoz Kholkabad in Samarkhand Oblast, Uzbekistan has more than 18 cotton harvesters per thousand hectares of cotton land. This is nearly 40 per cent above the average for the republic. Still only 63 per cent of the cotton at this Kolkhoz was harvested mechanically. The proportion must be lower for an average Kolkhoz. The authors were actually able to observe large numbers of Kolkhozniki, frequently women, picking cotton.
7. For the two Central Asian republics not included in Table 4.2 the relative costs of production in 1976 were as follows (in rubles per ton):

	Kolkhozy	Sovkhozy
Kirghiz SSR	353	414
Turkmen SSR	483	509

(Source: *NK SU 60*)

It, therefore, appears that for the Central Asia as a whole the cost of production at the Sovkhozy was higher than that at the Kolkhozy by something like 5 per cent.
8. As we have already stated, we do not know what items are included in

cost and how they are evaluated. There seems to be dissatisfaction expressed in Soviet writings on the appropriateness of the profit measures based on such cost calculations. See, for example, L. Kassirov, 'The Profitability of Socialist Agriculture' in *Problems of Economics*, October 1977 (translated from *Voprosy Economiki*, 1977, No. 4) which concludes: 'Thus the existing profitability calculation methods, which are based on the evaluation of production according to a system of zonal purchase prices and on the *incomplete consideration of the resources* used, significantly limit the possibility for using this indicator for the planned management of agriculture.' (Emphasis added.)

9. See Chapter 2 for the numerous qualifications.

10. These facts emerged through the discussion the authors had with the staff members of the Central Asian Institute of Scientific Research on Agricultural Economy, Tashkent.

11. It appears that in many areas in Central Asia grain is grown on marginal land. The authors were repeatedly told that the relatively low output of grain per hectare is due to conditions such as dry farming.

12. Once again the reader must note the strong warning sounded in an earlier chapter about the likely error in these measurements due to the problems of comparability of quality and various other factors and the disclaimer that these comparisons should not be interpreted as the suggestion that adopting international prices would be optimal. The only reason we are using the international prices is that we have no other standard with which to compare the procurement prices. At best such comparison reveals what is the relative reward of producing cotton and grain as compared to what such rewards would be if the growers could sell internationally at the ruling prices (which are assumed to be constant but, in reality, would be affected by the entry of a new seller of substantial size).

13. *Net* Soviet exports were 27 per cent of domestic production in 1976. In the context of the point discussed here gross exports seem to be more relevant, however.

14. This appears to be a reasonable assumption for the major part of the cotton export in view of the fact that, e.g., in 1976, only about 40 per cent of Soviet cotton exports were sold to the COMECON countries. In recent years France and Japan together have bought about a quarter.

15. These all USSR data do not constitute a convincing evidence of the decline in the personal plots. Compare, for example, the data shown in Morosov, *Soviet Agriculture*, Moscow 1977. The contribution of personal plots in marketed output of all crops declined from 13 per cent in 1940 to 11 per cent in 1960 and 10 per cent in 1975. In view of the steady decline in the labour intensity of agriculture over the period such minor reduction is probably quite consistent with the fairly rapid increase in the output of personal plot per household. In meat, milk and poultry the share declined more sharply. But these are the sectors in which collective agriculture experienced a phenomenal acceleration in growth in recent decades and new technology is frequently more suitable to large-scale production.

16. At the huge Tashkent Kolkhoz Market the authors saw tomatoes selling at 12 kopecs per kilogramme at the state shop (located inside the market) and at 60 to 70 kopecs at the stalls set up by the Kolkhozniki. The quality difference was striking. For cucumber the price difference was 50 per cent and quality difference was less striking.

17. At the Dushanbe Kolkhoz Market the authors saw the Kolkhozniki selling a wide variety of home-made goods – for example, honey, jam and jelly.

18. There is considerable theoretical literature concerning the allocation of labour between collective and personal land in a Soviet-type Kolkhoz under alternative assumptions about the behaviour of the entities involved. The interested reader is referred to: E. D. Domar, 'The Soviet Collective Farm as a Producer's Co-operative', *American Economic Review* (September 1966, Walter Oi and Elizabeth Clayton, 'A Peasant's View of a Soviet Collective Farm', *American Economic Review*, March 1968 and Michael Bradley, 'Incentives and Labour Supply on Soviet Collective Farms' in *Canadian Journal of Economics*, August 1971. It is useful to note that, contrary to what some people think, the personal plots are not frowned upon by the Kolkhoz. Indeed, the personal plots receive a good deal of help from the Kolkhoz and from state investment in agriculture in the form of fodder, fertiliser, services of equipment, transport services, extension services and other inputs.

CHAPTER 5

1. These figures were supplied to the authors by the Kolkhoz department of the Ministry of Agriculture, Uzbekistan.

2. Note, however, that tying taxes to profits may easily produce a perverse result by inducing the Kolkhoz to pay high incomes to workers and report low profit. Kolkhoz XXII Party Congress paid more than 85 per cent of value added to the Kolkhozniki. This is way above the average 66 per cent ratio obtaining in the other four collective farms.

3. As the authors found, it is usual for the Kolkhoz management to organise such work in slack seasons. They provide transport to take 'surplus' workers to construction sites and generally try to take advantage of lucrative outside work by making internal adjustments.

4. The authors visited a number of kindergartens and schools in the five Kolkhozy. To give some idea of a typical kindergarten, the Kolkhoz Karl Marx provided facilities for 50 children between ages 3 and 6 years. They were divided into two groups, each looked after by a teacher and a nurse. It being the season for picking cotton the kindergarten hours were from 8 a.m. to 8 p.m.

CHAPTER 6

1. Note, however, that there is no need for the intensity of outside employment per person to be the same as that for Kolkhoz employment.

We have no estimate of the intensity of outside employment.

2. At the Central Asian Institute of Scientific Research on the Agricultural Economy the authors were told that this system was instituted in March 1965 to replace a past system of incentive payments. At present cotton, wheat, rice, meat, wool and milk are covered by such a system of incentive payments.

3. In one of the farms – Kolkhabad, we were told of the periodic existence of zvenos.

Index

age distribution, 10
agriculture, procurement prices, 22–
5, 31–3, 36; incomes in, 28–30, 32;
production, 33; retail prices, 36;
investment in, 49–50, 79; and taxation, 78–9; growth of, 102–3;
official policy on, 104
All-Union Congress of Collective
Farmers, 2nd (1935), 40; 3rd
(1969), 43
Andijan Oblast, 1
artels, *see* kolkhozy

bais (feudal landowners), 37
birth rate, 7–11, 90–1
Bokhara, 70
Bokhara Emirate, 2

capital, and state control, 21; and
agricultural trade, 36; and kolkhozy, 49; in Sovkhozy, 66; and
credit, 79
cattle, 69, 98; *see also* livestock
collective farms, *see* kolkhozy
Communist Party of the Soviet
Union, 46, 51
consumption, social, 81–2, 84, 88–
9, 105; *see also* Public Consumption Fund
cost of living, 30, 33, 35
cotton, early development, 2; and
industrialisation, 13; production,
21–2, 25–7, 31, 62–8, 72, 84, 92–
3, 97, 103; procurement prices,
21–6, 31–3, 47, 68, 70–3, 92–3,
97; specialisation encouraged, 26,
28, 68, 103; labour requirements,
27–8, 68–9; labour costs, 66; ex-

ports, 73; and incomes, 94, 93;
quality differences, 92–3, hand-
picking, 110 n26, 113 n6
credit, 49–50, 53, 61, 79–80

death rate, 7–9
dekhans (peasants), 37
delivery quotas, 21
doctors, 20; *see also* health services
Dushanbe, Tajikistan, 91, 115 n16

earnings, *see* income
education, achievements in, 18–20,
105; post-war expansion, 52; expenditure on, 88–9, 95, 99, 102;
see also literacy

family allowances, 89
Ferghana Oblast, 1, 70
Five-Year Plan, First (1929), 38
food prices, 34–5
Frunze, 107 n7

gas (natural), 13
grain, procurement prices, 22–5,
31–3, 47, 70–3, 116 n2; sown area,
25–6, 72, 97; production, 26–7,
70, 72–5, 98; labour requirements, 27–8, 69

health services, 20, 88, 95, 99, 105
hospitals, 20
hydroelectricity (HEP), 13

immigration, 9, 12, 67

117

D5